New Thinking
for a
New Millennium

The Processes and Application of Abstracting

New Thinking for a New Millennium

The Processes and Application of Abstracting

Dr. William J. Williams

Pentland Press, Inc.
England • USA • Scotland

Also by the Author:

General Semantics and the Social Sciences
Uncommon Sense and Dimensional Awareness
Epistemics: Personalizing the Process of Change
Semantic Behavior and Decision Making
Selections from Semantic Behavior and Decision Making
The Miracle of Abduction

PUBLISHED BY PENTLAND PRESS, INC.
5122 Bur Oak Circle, Raleigh, North Carolina 27612
United States of America
919-782-0281

ISBN 1-57197-173-4
Library of Congress Catalog Card Number 99-070437

Copyright © 1999 William J. Williams
All rights reserved, which includes the right to reproduce this book or portions
thereof in any form whatsoever except as
provided by the U.S. Copyright Law.

Printed in the United States of America

Contents

Foreword . . . .*vii*

Preface . . . .*ix*

Acknowledgments . . . .*xiii*

Introduction . . . .*xv*

The Second Introduction: Don't Ask Why . . . . *xxiii*

Part One: Background . . . .*xxv*

Chapter One
    Correspondence: Structural Similarity—The What (Primary) 1

Chapter Two
    Correspondence: Structural Similarity—The How (Secondary) . .9

Chapter Three
    The Verb "To Be:" Fundamental Focus—The Use of 19

Chapter Four
    Epistemological Background for Knowing and Naming 23

Part Two: Implementation: The Processes of Abstracting *41*

Introduction *43*

Chapter Five
    Orders of Abstraction—A Diagnosis
    Propositions and Propositional Functions 45

Chapter Six
    Types of Abstracting: Diagnosis, Evaluation and Analysis 53

Chapter Seven
    Levels of Abstracting: Analysis 59

Chapter Eight
    Fusion: Integration and Rigorous Analysis 67

Chapter Nine
    The Style 83

Epilogue *85*

Glossary of Terms *87*

References *93*

Index *95*

Foreword

Few researchers in the earthy field of public administration, a science that focuses on what government actually does, or rather how the public bureaucracy works in practice, dwell on the epistemology of what they do and how they think about what they do. Dr. Williams, following Alfred Korzybski and J. Samuel Bois, has spent much of his academic career occupied with the epistemology of knowledge and learning and the scrupulous use of language in expressing thoughts. This book follows on from his previous publications—*The Miracle of Abduction, Semantic Behavior and Decision Making, Epistemics, Uncommon Sense and Dimensional Awareness,* and *General Semantics and the Social Sciences*—and concerns itself with applied epistemology or the epistemics of pursuing new knowledge and the art of abstraction, particularly the way we think about thinking. Becoming more aware of our own processes of abstracting helps us understand the way we think as we do and how we judge things; it takes us well beyond classic Cartesian quantification and mathematical expressions so familiar to researchers everywhere. These are fundamentally static abstractions, which like snapshot photographs cannot convey the continuous motion of life, movement, development, progression, or qualitative improvement, let alone something novel never before discovered by human beings.

In this book, Dr. Williams discusses stages of abstracting, commencing with sensing (primitive realism). He moves through classifying and all of its manifestations, ultimately reaching the most sophisticated processes of integrating and postulating. His compact writing style demands a high level of concentration and considerable thinking; especially in regard to nonlinear thinking where original thinkers make leaps of faith by imagining a different order of

New Thinking For A New Millennium

perception. While we still do not know quite how to teach this novel type of thinking, along with Albert Einstein, Dr. Williams agrees that there is no more important activity than getting people to think and think about thinking.

Gerald Caiden, Ph.D.
University of Southern California

Preface

Many professional scientists and people in general continue to structure their processes in terms of "framework," either/or, and interaction. Framework is a static concept, while interaction is a mechanical concept, and either/or is rigid and Aristotelian. In the case of the latter, it manifests itself as: waves or particles; with mass or without mass; and contracting or expanding. By definition, it is more appropriate to couch these as: mass-not much mass, particles-waves, contracting-expanding. The simple use of the hyphen creates a different epistemic focus and mindset.

My observations have revealed that this simple process is overlooked in some of the most advanced writings, ideas, and findings. For example, Stephen Hawking, in writing his *Brief History of Time*, used the either/or and framework modes. The question posed in this manner would naturally lead one to reach a certain answer. For example: is the universe expanding or contracting? It is not a question, it seems to me, that should be posed. We now know epistemologically, that they both are cut from the "same cloth." The universe is both expanding and contracting. Again, we know this from waves and particles, that it is both and not one or the other. Yet, when new questions are posed, some will still, even in science, use the rigid framework of structural thinking. It is still a mystery to me as to why Hawking, with all of this brilliance, would pose questions in such an Aristotelian fashion. As I stated earlier, in his *Brief History of Time*, there are examples of static either/or thinking. Einstein, of course, had a similar difficulty, and, so did Alfred Korzybski. The difference is that Korzybski acknowledged that he had the difficulty.

I had difficulty understanding the notion of mass or not mass in the Neutrino being used to find out whether the universe was expanding or

New Thinking For A New Millennium

contracting. As I said earlier, contracting and expanding should not have been the structure. The goal should have been how the contracting and expanding occurs. Then, the notion of mass or nonmass in the neutrino would have been moot. The asking of the question differently would have taken us in a different direction. The focusing on mass would have been declared a degree question rather than a difference in kind, and it possibly could have served to produce information relative to something else, rather than contracting and expanding.

What I am finding is that the greatest of minds are locked into this fixed thinking, and it intrudes as they perform their tasks. The simplicity of this boggles my mind. This simple focus seems to elude us as we approach the most complex questions. The remedy is so obvious that we miss it. Transcending this rigid pattern might hold a key to the success of our work—a simple epistemological focus that shifts us from the either-or to nonfragmentation. The question, in political, social, economical, philosophical, psychological, or scientific matter, has to be what is going on, not is it this or that, guilty or innocent, right or wrong, expanding or contracting, sink or swim, old or young, or love or hate. Transcending the old structure is the "real" task. How to do it is the "real" question.

The purpose of this book is to suggest a method that leans in that direction—a method that does not eliminate the old structure but clarifies its role and shows how the new emerges automatically as we clarify the role of the old.

In 1933 Werner Heisenberg invited Neils Bohr, his son Christian, Felix Black, and Carl Friedrich for a skiing holiday in the village of Bayrischzell on the southern slope of Grome Traithern. While there, they had a discussion about how to describe findings in physics and astronomy. They concluded that they quite unthinkingly used the concepts of classical physics as if they had never known the limitations of these concepts. They also concluded that, while they established laws that differ from classical physics, they were forced to use ordinary language to speak of everyday experience. They agreed that this language was inadequate, and necessary if they were going to communicate their results effectively.

In the *Los Angeles Times* on 15 June 1998, in an article titled "Missing Pieces of the Cosmic Puzzle," it was concluded that we are still faced with the same difficulty. Physicists, now, who study the universe, are heard using terms like "quintessence," "dark matter," "smooth stuff," "funny energy," and "tangled strings." The physicists

Dr. William J. Williams

continue to speak in tongues, struggling to invent an appropriate language, but for the time being they sound more like wordsmiths than scientists. This manuscript is an attempt to shed some light on this difficulty.

Likewise, the other professions and ordinary citizens are locked into this pervasive and obsolete methodological mindset. Therefore, this new direction is essential here also.

Acknowledgments

Many people have contributed to the production of this manuscript. I am grateful to Ms. Lydia Smith of Australia for her editing, typing, organizing, writing technique, rearranging much of the manuscript and development of the elaborate index; Ms. Artimese Porter, our office administrator, who has typed and retyped the manuscript at least five times; Dr. Keith Devlin, author of *Goodbye Descartes* and *Language at Work,* for reading portions of the manuscript and making suggestions; Dr. Bart Kosko, author of *Fuzzy Thinking,* for reading parts of the manuscript and recommending some changes; Helga Tawll, my former teaching assistant and friend, who has been helpful in many ways and designed the cover for this book. Last, but by no means least, I am grateful to Rex Hunter, the movie producer, for suggesting the title for the book.

Introduction

There are several ideas we must pursue if we are to create a rigorous, qualitative process for analyzing, examining and evaluating issues. First, the process has to make particular cases of disciplines. In other words, we cannot build a viable process by identifying one discipline as being separate from any area of concentration. Psychology, physics, biology, mathematics, philosophy, and economics have commonalities at the lowest order of abstraction and submicroscopic process (the event). The disciplines come from one big mass. It is only at the highest orders of abstraction that we separate conceptually, categorize, classify, fragment, and label. There is no fragmenting and categorizing at the event order. To be able to effectively embrace the event order, the usage of the terms multidisciplinary and interdisciplinary must be replaced by a nondisciplinary approach, or epistemic analysis, which emphasizes a focusing on the epistemological underpinnings that give rise to the various disciplines.

Analytically, most of the time we do some categorizing and classifying. However, it is not whether we classify, but how we classify. By definition, theory construction is analytical. We use language and symbols. The language and symbols ought to be adequate and represent our thinking at the very lowest and fundamental part of abstracting, so that we might capture submicroscopic "stirrings." By capturing the submicroscopic "stirrings," we cease making a distinction between the disciplines. Disciplines are not separate and distinct, and any message to the contrary, for the most part, appears to be faulty.

Secondly, we must recognize the need for a new language. It is erroneous to assume that we can take old categories and represent new ideas and findings. If we do use old categories, we proceed to build paradigms with an inappropriate language. This is where the so-called

New Thinking For A New Millennium

scientific process has been strong. The scientific process, though awkward at times, has focused frequently on introducing a new language and methodology when and wherever new ideas are introduced. In most disciplines, we assume that the old mechanism and language are appropriate, and we launch the discussion of new ideas without addressing the most fundamental issue: the language we use to design our constructs.

Thirdly, there is a focus on rigor, but a particular kind of rigor. If the rigorous discussion is about using old quantitative methodology, separating qualitative from quantitative, systems from reduction, phenomenology from epistemology, we maroon ourselves. A valid and appropriate rigor engages how we ought to view these terms and whether they are useful. If the rigor is to have value, it must be usable by all disciplines since all emanate from a similar source. One can be rigorous logically and mechanically and accept the old assumptions, or one can be rigorous at a more appropriate stage of development. Rigor, in the latter sense, would be a meticulous analysis of the language we use, as Arthur Bentley proposed in *Linguistic Analysis of Mathematics and Knowing and the Known*.

The rigor must also take the shape of exploring new aspects of thinking, which also ultimately takes us to the language that we use. It is fundamental to our process. The emphasis on language and meticulous analysis raises two ancillary questions: what criteria do I use for making my analysis, and how should it now be characterized or symbolized? Most of the progress made in certain rigorous areas that communicate a degree of adequacy is the result of an effort to identify and change the fundamental methodological process. The progress is also signified by paradigm proposals, not merely by talk about paradigms. In other words, one should focus on a methodology for achieving results and develop a set of criteria for making judgments about that methodology and results. When Einstein moved from Newtonian physics to relativity, a new system was introduced with a new language.

When Max Planck moved into quantum physics, a whole new language was introduced. Although all of these systems had similarities, they were treated as belonging to different orders of thinking. Differences as well as similarities were communicated. To devise a new structurally appropriate, rigorous language is a difficult task. The question at this juncture is not whether, but how? This writing, then, would be without real merit and fraudulent if I did not attempt to share

Dr. William J. Williams

with you a fundamental methodological process that might shed some light on how we might become more linguistically rigorous. A word of caution again: this would not be rigor for "social science" or "natural science," but a nondisciplinary kind of rigor that applies to all disciplines and automatically makes a particular case of disciplines within an overarching process—a kind of rigor that emphasizes the need for accurately and adequately creating a symbolically structured correspondence to the world of events. The construct of central concern to this symbolic correspondence is *applied epistemology* or *epistemics*. The methods designed to bring about this correspondence and provide us with the skill for rigorous qualitative analysis are the processes of abstracting. Simultaneously using as backdrop these perspectives: macroscopic, microscopic, and submicroscopic.

By utilizing the processes of abstracting, we are able to identify the commonalities of thinking and creative functioning shared by all disciplines. We will pinpoint similarities and differences in terms of our abstracting methodological focus while we study abstracting as a method for examining abstracting and subject matters. For our purpose, abstracting will be approached as orders, levels, types, and styles. The style and sophistication of the person, along with the peculiar characteristics of the discipline involved, will determine to some extent how the processes of abstracting are applied.

The abstracting overarching process being used is automatically arranged to determine our focus. From this overarching format will also emerge new ways of viewing and naming, since the methodology in the overarching process is similar to the natural functioning of the underlying process. Similar to, but not the same as, the overarching process is analytical and the underlying process is synthetic. We are examining these different "levels" simultaneously: the underlying process, the human-made and labeled discipline, and the theoretical inquiry process. In other words, we are thinking about our thinking in a self-reflexive manner. The abstracting process results in the production of new ways of viewing old categories and the invention of new namings. It is a self-correcting process that requires immersion rather than mechanical "tinkering." Emergence, transformation, evolving, and transactions are the key terms to describe what takes place. In simple terms, it is a "transactional" process. The description used here is a crude attempt to describe the nondescribable. It is drawn hierarchically. In actuality, it is more like a "spider's web," which in this instance gives birth to a thought, idea, or direction. The mechanical way of viewing this is one way of utilizing the processes as tools to communicate verbally—to some extent, the abductive process. It requires rising to an overarching level of involvement which does not separate natural and social sciences. This new focus does not classify phenomena as social or scientific. The classifications are of different orders, levels, and types of abstracting and are called applied epistemology or epistemics.

It is important to understand the intricacies involved in the processes of abstracting. We abstract each and every day. However, few are aware of the processes taking place. The awareness, understanding, and application of these processes are ultimately sought through this document. Consciousness of the abstracting processes has real bearing on how we behave and function. Through the processes of abstracting, we will be able to dissect and meticulously analyze phenomena. Moreover, by using these processes and by partially focusing on the language, we will be able to better define ourselves and our internal "thinking" structures.

Abstracting appears to be an undergirding human function which, before 1933, was not defined as a structured process. It was not seen as a natural biological and thinking process. Now we look upon the abstracting process as a method to understand and use. Previously, we defined abstracting as a noun (abstraction) which is static and formistic. Abstracting as a verb introduces processes. It becomes something we do, and it transcends the law of the excluded middle and the laws of noncontradiction and identity. For example, the separation between line and staff is erased. They both are and are not at the same time. Nevertheless, qualitative differences are meticulously and precisely identified by using the processes.

Intricacies of Language

There is a tremendous difference between thinking in verbal terms and contemplating nonverbally. Searching for the proper structure of language to fit thinking and the nonverbal level can be exceedingly difficult. This difficulty is compounded by the personal history one brings to the search.

However, when we correctly abstract, the latter will be minimized as long as we realize and accept that we will never be done with the process. There are an infinite number of characteristics to observe and clarify for any given situation or idea, making our approach never-ending. Becoming conscious of your own abstracting and seeing the

Dr. William J. Williams

importance of this awareness plays a primary role in thinking and making better judgments.

What we abstract is never a mirror image of what is going on (WIGO), but an interpretation of the transaction between the atomic going on and the outside psychophysiological responses. By being concerned about the healthy functioning of our nervous systems, we can move from being solely occupied with the satisfaction of lower-order needs, which are truly "selfish" (e.g., give me, feed me, love me), to the additional concerns for the satisfaction of our higher needs which can be accomplished only by being selfish at a higher level (Weinberg 1955). However, neither exists or functions entirely isolated from the other. We move from a higher order to a lower one. We abstract whatever we can, and according to the degree of our intelligence and the information we have, we summarize, generalize, and integrate.

The awareness of language we use must be a part of our attention to inquiry from moment to moment automatically. Consequently, it is not appropriate to isolate language as a particular field of inquiry. It must be a part of our desire to think more coherently about broad questions concerning worldviews and methodologies. Additionally, a part of our task is to understand better how the ordinary mode of language functions, so that we may be able to use even the ordinary more coherently. Central is a focus on the nonordinary and ordinary, along with a rejection of the division between language and thought, which will aid us in rising above fragmentation.

The rigorous qualitative process in the document breaks down as follows:

1. Correspondence: structural similarity—the what (primary)
2. Correspondence: tructural similarity—the how (secondary)
3. The verb "to be": a fundamental focus
4. Epistemological background and guide for knowing and naming
5. Orders of abstraction: diagnosis
6. Types of abstracting: diagnosis and evaluation
7. Levels of abstracting: analysis
8. Fusion: integration and rigorous analysis
9. Styles

New Thinking For A New Millennium

This rigorous qualitative analysis is not in opposition to quantitative analysis, nor is it necessarily in lieu of it. It is in conjunction with it. Accordingly, quantitative can be a particular case within qualitative epistemology, and qualitative can be a particular case of quantitative—in the latter case, however, only when defined within the boundaries of a structure and not epistemologically, as a rearrangement of structure.

We must rise to a level where judgment and recommending may be made in a more inclusive manner. Quantitative analysis does not enable us to do that unless it is a part of larger epistemological concerns, as with Bertrand Russell's theory of types; that is, propositions and propositional functions. Therefore, for our purpose here, we will merely refer to quantitative as a particular case within rigorous qualitative processes.

We often talk about the integration and synthesizing of knowledge, disciplines, ideas, theories, and policies. In my judgment, we cannot integrate unless we have something that enables us to do it. The process in this book is an attempt to communicate that something. That something emerges as processes of abstracting. It is necessary to be holistic, but also to dissect and cut things up into pieces for a more rigorous analysis, and simultaneously at another level, visualize those pieces as a whole and connect the lines mentally; that is, never isolating without holding as a constant how the isolates are connected. The chapter on fusion of orders, levels, types, and styles will focus on this as a theme. Alfred Korzybski would call this nonelementalistic. I call it nonlogical. I separate, for convenience, thinking as follows: illogical, logical, and nonlogical.

The illogical (a system without a system) is pre-Aristotelian. The logical (syllogistic reasoning) is Aristotle, Descartes, and so on, and the nonlogical (Einstein, Planck), qualitative analysis, the focus of this book.

Keith Devlin, a mathematician at Stanford's Center for the Study of Language and Communication, wrote a book called *Goodbye Descartes*. In that book he said, in essence, that we want to say goodbye to Cartesian thinking and come up with a new way of understanding the world that transcends mathematics and the old ways of science and disciplines. He proposed the term soft mathematics for the part of the new way of thinking that corresponds to the current mathematical approach. To transcend mathematics and continue using the term, one is a paradox, and two, a new process, deserves a new meaning and new

Dr. William J. Williams

labels. Einstein used relativity rather than Newtonian physics plus gravitation and electromagnetism, and Bois started using epistemics in order to transcend general semantics. Keith Devlin said we needed to have a new framework. Framework being "static," I would rather use process. However, Devlin himself concentrates on processing in another recent book—*Language at Work,* written in collaboration with sociologist Duska Rosenberg. A part of Devlin's focus in *Goodbye Descartes* is about outlook and perspective, and what he called our way of looking at the world. We agree on this point, and also that an additional emphasis has to be on method. While he did not focus there in *Goodbye Descartes,* he did so in his *Language At Work.* We could all agree that we want to get from California to New York in four hours, but if we use the train or automobile, we will not get there in four hours, at least not in 1999. We must take a jet plane as our method. The same applies with our new process, perspective or worldview. We can agree on the worldview, but unless we couple it with a new method, the new views cannot be implemented. May I say also, at this juncture, that the method is as important as the perspective or worldview. They are part and parcel of each other. An inappropriate method does not enable us to accomplish the task. Although Devlin mentions Aristotle's syllogistic reasoning and soft mathematics in his book, he agrees with my view that we cannot go back to those methods, because they tend to be inappropriate for the implementation of fresh and new ideas. The thrust must be forward.

The Second Introduction
Don't Ask Why

The Why Questions

The why question is expressed with impunity. It is the poorest way to ask a question. The why question is a "bonehead" question unless it is used to inquire about why, as in never say never and always avoid always. Thus, the use of the word why to ask about why is legitimate, as is the use of is to talk about is. For example, it is unwise to use is, meaning that it is unwise to use why, never and always at certain levels of abstracting and in some orders of abstraction. It is sufficient to deal with this formulation by expressing the reason in a one-liner, since I have dealt with the question in depth in other places. The why question, epistemologically speaking, is behind many of our difficulties and unfortunately provides a foundation for our linguistics and speech forms. The *why* question and *is* are one and the same and this foundation permeates our thinking, and thus our decisionmaking. It is Aristotelian. Other forms of speech and grammar may be more adequate than our English. Classical English is inappropriate simply because it "sports" the is. It would be politically unacceptable to push this point too far because this particular philosophical grammatical process, to some extent, serves as a foundation for our culture and thinking. The urge to have everyone speak and use the classical language may be politically, socially, and practically correct, but it is inappropriate for making good decisions and understanding the world and ourselves. In short, the political and socially correct approach may be detrimental to the human condition but all right for "commercial" success. The Indo-European countries are imbued with a process that may be inadequate for sound human progress. Consequently, "ebonics" and "Hopi," as well as some other structures, may be better. You can say, "I said it" and "it was said here." The ignorance that emerges from our enamorment with the

New Thinking For A New Millennium

existing grammatical structure is rampant. The "ebonics" people could easily make the point that their format features a system more in keeping with appropriate good sense because it eschews the uses of why on many levels, but the limitation does not provide us with an appropriate structure. In short, the is and why, on some levels, are the villains.

Part One:

Background

Chapter One

Correspondence: Structural Similarity—The What (Primary)

A structural similarity to the world of events is the phrase that guides our theory about correspondence. The crucial issue is the assumption that correspondence can be accomplished. The assumption is not without merit, because we can cite examples of inferences that have been drawn from several disciplines. These instances, up to now, indicate a degree of accuracy. Some notable examples are gravitation, relativity, quantum, nonlogical thinking, Gestalt, transformation, and circular responses.

Mathematicians, no matter how important their work, have never gone so far as to appreciate fully that they are producing an ideal human relational language of structure similar to that of the world and to that of the human nervous system, according to Dr. Kosko in *Fuzzy Thinking*.

In the evolution of mathematics, we find that the ratios of greater, equal, and less precise numbers comparison is the simplest form of evolution, the first being a search for relations and the second a discovery of exact relations. This process of search for relations and structure appears to be inherent and natural in humans. It has led not only to the discovery of numbers but has also shaped their two aspects, namely the cardinal and the ordinal aspects. Relations are obviously highly important tools for exploring the structure of the world, since structure can be analyzed in terms of relations.

These appear to be related to the structure of the human nervous system, which abstracts, generalizes, or integrates in higher orders and finds similarities. Our task is to advance a language structure that represents the relations and structure. We begin with the notion that words are not objects. This expresses a structural fact. This idea renders *the is of identity* as unconditionally false. The general structure of our

New Thinking For A New Millennium

language invites "identification." Even science is not free from "identification," but "identification" simply vanishes when we cease confusing orders of abstraction. The semantic difficulties in the foundation of mathematics, including the problem of infinity, the irrational number, the difficulties of the Einstein theories, quantum, radius of the universe, and infinite velocities, are mainly due to semantic blockages or a commitment to the structure of the old language. (See my Preface for an example of this.)

If we abolish the "is of identity," we become adequate in the mathematical language of function. This appears similar to the structure of the world descriptively and similar to the logical nervous process.

The empirical world is such in structure (by inspection) that we can add, subtract, multiply, and divide. However, a language able to deal with additive, simple, immediate, and unimportant issues is entirely unfit structurally, to deal with the complex processes, which underlie the most fundamental difficulties of life. It is in physics only, since Einstein, that we have begun to see that the primitive, simplest, and easiest to sense linear equations are not structurally adequate. The universal character is change, motion, waves, and particles. A language of similar structure must have means to deal with such relations.

This is somewhat of a restrictive view of mathematics, but it appears at times we emphasize, up to a point, mathematical language, which means numbers and arithmetical language, the theory of function, the differential and integral calculus, and different geometries. The science of physics originated with the introduction of differential equations, which eliminated semantic disturbances, namely, "identification" and "elementalism."

I have talked about relations and functions. There is another term that is closely related. The term is transformation. We say that we have transformed a into b or vice versa. This implies a relationship between a and b, which is established by transformation.

This is related to higher abstractions being translated physiologically into lower abstractions, and the dynamic into static and vice versa. Transformation reconciles higher-order and lower-order abstractions. To facilitate this qualitatively we use *levels* and *types* of abstracting to examine *orders* of abstraction.

The whole of modern physics became possible through calculus and the different orders of abstraction, which our nervous structure produces and which are reflected in the very structure of our methods of mathematics. However, the power of analysis in our higher-order

Dr. William J. Williams

abstractions is due precisely to the fact that they are static. The lower orders are nonpermanent and shifting, and evade serious analysis. If y is said to be a function of x, where x is given in symbols, we write $y = f(x)$, which we read as y is equal to a function of x, or y is equal to f of x, if y is a function of x or $y = f(x)$. Then, x is the independent variable, and we arbitrarily assign values. Y is dependent on the value of x.

Orders of abstraction are dependent variables, and *levels* and *types* are independent variables. Thus, we see how the notion of calculus matches the language of abstracting. Once we assign weights to x, we can determine something about y. If we assign $x = 5$ between that, we can assign many values, and as 1, 2, 3, 4, 5, or 1, 1Ω, 2, 2Ω, and so on, or 1°, 1Ω, 1æ, 2, and so on. We turn abstractions from propositional functions to propositions. The points I am making here are not just about computation, but about semantic states: how to develop language in keeping with natural processes; how the adaptation of the calculus language creates a structural relationship to the nervous system and the world of events; and how language helps us to recognize difficulties in policies and decisionmaking. With the semantic states, we create the mathematics and, epistemologically, mathematicians do it with numbers and other abstract entities. Non-mathematicians can do it with the "nonidentity" language, which is based on the "same" epistemological underpinning.

A mechanical method to aid us is the notion of *multiordinality*. It is a logical system symbol. Multiordinality is designed to precision our thinking, in order to have our analysis enable us to make a "propositional function" a "proposition." For example, with orders of abstraction, we have propositional functions and low-order and high-order abstractions, which is in keeping with the calculus notion of function as a dependent variable. *Levels of abstracting* (which has as a submethod, multiordinality) becomes the independent variable, and we are well on our way to analysis, and imputing substance to the orders as in $y = f(x)$ then $f(x) = y$. After the assignment of weights and values, we have expressed the calculus notion of transformation and introduced relation. This is a part of the structure of the semantic state.

The structure of the semantic state becomes a factor in the development of a structure with correspondence. Whether it is dealt with mathematically or nonmathematically, one can produce the other. It is not chicken or egg, It is egg = chicken, chicken = egg. The translation from lower to higher and higher to lower is about the semantic process. If we use mathematical symbols, the same as $y = f(x)$,

New Thinking For A New Millennium

and there is a semantic blockage in the assignment of values, then the results will not yield proper conceptualization. Likewise, if the semantic blockage occurs from logic, the translation (the processes of abstracting) will not correspond to the natural structure. Linear logic is the "is of identification" and commitment to the structure of an old language. The *theory of types* as undergirded by calculus, an expression of the processes of abstracting (orders of abstraction), was an attempt to create better correspondence. It sought to show how we move from one order to another. Correspondence, in this instance, is a distinction between proposition and propositional function. This is crucial to public policy analysis. The orders provide, however, only a first step. A proper semantic state, as provided by the *theory of types*, can be illustrated in this way: Joe says all Cretians are liars. Joe is a Cretian. Does that make Joe a liar? Not necessarily. Joe is standing outside the class. He is not a member of the class in this instance when Joe talks about Cretians, he is not speaking as a Cretian. A class is different from its members. The barber shaves everyone in town who does not shave himself. When he shaves himself he is not a barber A class of barbers is different from its members, and so he does shave himself. *A* is *a* and non-*a*. All propositions must be in some way limited before becoming a *legitimate totality*. Any limitation which makes it legitimate must make any statement about the *totality* fall outside the totality. There must not be *illegitimate totalities*. Ambiguity and *vicious circle fallacies* have to do with including *illegitimate totalities* in the argument; for example, when a statement is about a statement, and one includes in the statement, the statement about the statement. The statement that the barber only shaves those who do not shave themselves is a propositional function and does not include the barber in the totality when values are assigned. The barber is exempt. The ingredient supplies us with an analytical process for determining structural correspondence with orders as nonself-subsistent. Orders historically have been used in this manner. Inherent are two dimensions: (1) the natural orders of the nervous system (a vertical representation), and (2) the distinction between propositions and propositional functions (which can be determined to some extent by the recognition of illegitimate totalities, et cetera). We, at this time, can add a structural correspondence by assuming orders to be propositional functions until a determination is made with the application of *levels* and *types* of abstracting (values and weights). This perspective is crucial since we are concerned with validity and "truth," and because in many instances orders will only produce validity.

Dr. William J. Williams

For structural similarity, we engage two dimensions—one of analysis and the other of what continues to linger behind the analysis. These are one and the same as we deal with the first and continue to elicit from the second. The process is circular. The key terms here are emergence, metamorphosis, transformation, and mutation. Therefore, in addition to the methodological analysis, we need to be grounded in a figurative background. That figurative background has some relationship to "science." The focus on "science" deserves some attention in order to create a proper focus. What do we mean by science? Our focus ought to be one that questions the formulation and epistemological underpinnings of science. It should be a focus that leads us into a questioning of using the term "science" or the developing of a process that addresses how scientific theories emerge. Our focus must be on questioning what has emerged in science.

For example, to just accept the results and the underpinnings of the law of aggregates and thus the notion of function, without questioning the notion, is not appropriate. However, if we focus on the things that give rise to aggregates and functions, we do not talk about "science" or borrowing, but rather about inventing and mutation. Consequently, in inventing, we do not imitate "science" as we know it but develop propositional functions that give rise to what we call science. Thus, we are not imitating but instead are creating. We then evaluate emergings and create for ourselves and science simultaneously. This is correspondence at a deeper level. Most of the information in "social science" is imitative. At a deeper level, we then begin to make recommendations for science. Since our level of involvement is about underpinnings, social science, policy, and so on become equals, not totally recipients of data and information from other disciplines. It is a vertical focus primarily, and horizontal secondarily.

A qualitative analysis ought to take the form of what may be enduring and lasting. There are some pervasive and invariant perspectives dictating the development of structures that are enduring. That perspective may be thinking and thinking about thinking. The secondary words may change; for example, leadership, economics, philosophy, man, woman, and freedom. How we think about those issues and what we call them at any given time may change depending upon findings. Qualitative analysis ought to identify the thinking process and develop structures that graphically depict how we operationalize that invisible process. This may be the crux of qualitative analysis. It should embrace the undergirding fundamentals.

New Thinking For A New Millennium

Quantitative analysis can deal with those secondary issues, but qualitative analysis, by definition, must have a deeper focus. In other words, multidisciplinary and interdisciplinary are secondary to nondisciplinary. By definition, nondisciplinary is qualitative in that it may dictate the ways and character of disciplines, multidisciplines, and interdisciplines. Whatever determines the survival of the disciplines must inevitably pose a challenge for inventing new ways of thinking about those subjects. The processes of abstracting enable us to determine the most basic enduring web of submicroscopic and microscopic activity; that is, those things that determine how we should view the interdisciplinary and multidisciplinary activity. This represents a move beyond fragmentation to holistic inquiry methods, which correspond to the structure of the world as we know it now in 1999.

An obvious example of the lack of structural correspondence is the U.S. Constitution, which emphasizes checks and balances. There is, as we know, a mechanical separation of the branches of government. The structure is based on Newtonian epistemology primarily. On the secondary level, the system is one of gross classifications. We know now that on both counts this system does not structurally correspond to the contemporary criteria and proper thinking. We know now that the holistic and organic perspectives are more appropriate for an understanding of the world. The balance of power syndrome violates these perspectives. We are given a structure that by definition does not enable us to become effective. It sets in motion a deleterious process fraught with unnecessary conflict leading to inefficiency and ineffectiveness in public policy. An organic system would be more desirable.

This mechanical constitutional system represents a propositional function masquerading as a proposition. Mechanically it has weights and values. On that level we have a proposition. There is validity. However, on the deeper level of "truth," it does not meet the criteria, meaning that in order for a proposition to be considered a "true" proposition, it must satisfy the criteria of validity and "truth." On the latter it falls short. This is based on the idea that "truth" is relative and it must represent what we know as "truth" at this time. The mechanical structure represents an obsolete "truth" and is superseded by a more current, organic, holistic, and Einsteinian epistemological focus rather than Newtonian. On the surface, with the use of orders of abstractions, the system of government emerges as a description one step from the first-order experience and appears to have all of the ingredients of a

Dr. William J. Williams

proposition. Then we apply *levels* of abstracting and find that we are at the *classifying* and *relating* levels. We then apply types of abstracting and find that the *classifying* and *relating* levels are obsolete. It would only be contemporary if it were of the *postulating* type. Our conclusions emerge automatically from our analysis, setting in motion transformation and emergence.

In conclusion: to have a structural correspondence, we utilize as the criteria up-to-date epistemological knowledge to identify validity, as well as "truths." If the subject lacks either, then it is a *contrary* rather than a *contradictory*. Once we use types to evaluate our orders, and then levels to analyze the results of types of abstracting, we can make the determination. These processes are used in conjunction with each other. The usage sets in motion what Mary Parker Follette referred to as the circular process. Hopefully, this perspective will bring us a step closer to understanding structural correspondence and how to approach it. Up to this point, we have dealt in a concrete manner, only with mechanical application of structural correspondence. We have left untouched the epistemological dimension of correspondence, which deals with the distinctions between validity and "truth." It is difficult to deal with the question of how to generate and invent the structures that produced Newtonian, Einsteinian and holistic ideas; that is, notions of relations, order, and function. However, if we focus on circularity, our chances improve.

Many parts of Einstein's theories of relativity were propositional functions. His observations about the velocity of light do not become propositions until experiments are conducted. The same applies to his *theory of local causes*. It did not become a proposition until the experiment; that is, an object in one place causes a similar object in another place 3,000 miles away to go up when the first object goes down. When the experiment was done, the theory became a proposition. Before it was done, it was a propositional function. The propositional function, at that point, is given values, weights, and measures, and so it is also with Korzybski's map versus territory analogy. Until we match the map with the territory, our map remains a propositional function. For example, we can draw a picture of the brain without ever seeing a brain. It is a propositional function until we observe it. Korzybski added something to the map-territory analogy, known as extensional devices. They are *dating, hyphens, indexing, plurals,* and *et cetera*. If we talk about a tax policy or a person ergo 1925, and it is 1999 when we decide to make application, we cannot consider what we say a proposition. It

New Thinking For A New Millennium

may have been a proposition in 1925, but in 1999 we must date and index. We must "extensionalize" the process. For example, we presently talk about the regulating of tobacco by using the analogy of prohibition against alcohol, which was largely unsuccessful. First of all, the analogy is dated and secondly, when we index, we find them different. Without drawing a new map about a similar territory, we run the risk of being *inaccurate* and *inadequate*. Consequently, we must apply the equation of propositional function versus proposition and not confuse the two. Moreover, we must invoke the postulating type of abstracting to examine and evaluate it. If we do not do this, we are merely using levels of abstracting, because the true situations may not be just a difference in degree (ergo levels). They may be a difference in kind (ergo types).

Chapter Two

Correspondence: Structural Similarity—The How (Secondary)

This brings us full circle, back to the notion of language, with an emphasis on nonfragmentation. A superficial examination shows that a key feature of fragmentation is the subject-verb-object structure. This structure implies that all action arises in a separate entity. There is, however, a different language structure, which is nonfragmentation. This nonfragmentation language has produced notions like gravitation, relativity, quantitative chaos and transaction and is a vehicle for the recognition of deeper emergings. The "magic" is in the "labeling." Therefore, we must be sure that whatever labels we produce are nonfragmenting and nonelementalistic. A key to understanding that something deeper, or the different language, is to observe how an understanding of the verb "to be" serves as a vehicle for translation and impacts the very generation of the ideas that emerge for possible transaction. For example, as Einstein had a notion of things being connected, like space and time, the translation became space-time, a linguistic change. However, simultaneously, we must be aware that the original idea behind space-time had to be influenced by a kind of thinking process we now call non-Aristotelian (nonelementalism and nonfragmentation). The point I am making here is that our immersion in the nonsubject–verb-object structure unconsciously produces holism, integration, and connectedness. This sets up an atmosphere for natural correspondence. However, the ideas are there at some deeper level, even when a proper structure is not introduced. What happens to these ideas that emerge without the benefit of a nonfragmentation structure? They are sometimes distorted. In some instances, they are not, because the notions of conscious nonfragmentation and nonelementalism came from some place. For example, if Planck was not consciously utilizing a non-Aristotelian process, "What happened?" Unconsciously,

New Thinking For A New Millennium

something was going on, which not only produced the idea, but also the language structure we identify as being important for the generation of the unconscious ideas. I have to tentatively conclude that despite the language structure, some persons are endowed with the ability to think on many different levels. They are automatically into correspondence about correspondence. Consciousness of this process has enabled those of us not endowed with the ability automatically to create a structural process that can be used to do what previously was done unconsciously; that is, we have identified it as the nonsubject–verb-predicate process. Mathematics is a good example of this.

A structural similarity can be found in the case of mathematics. Mathematics establishes a linguistic relational pattern without specific content. The noncontent character partially accounts for the generality of mathematical application. This noncontent is expressed in not assigning definite meanings to the undefined terms in mathematical postulates that have variable meanings which serve as propositional functions. Mathematics eschews the common sense language. Mathematics formulates something that is going on inside our skin on the unspeakable level. The unspeakable is the key, but before we focus on the unspeakable that produced the mathematics, I would like to discuss more about mathematics as a language.

The theory of aggregates and theory of groups are the mechanisms by which all languages, not only mathematics, have been built. They represent the most powerful and successful attempts at building exact relational languages.

The theory of aggregates underlies the theory of function. It includes all entities to which a certain characteristic belongs, and no entity without this characteristic belongs to the system, (Korzybski 1933).

Properly, simultaneously, the notion of group is a part of the process. The concept of group is associated and connected with the notions of transformation and invariance. If 1 is a number and 2 is a number, the operation t transforms 1 into 3 since $1 + 2 = 3$. But 3 has the character of being a number, so this characteristic is preserved and remains invariant. We are in contact with two notions, namely transformation and invariance, with the first implying chance and the other lack of chance or permanence. The world, ourselves included, can be analyzed in terms of transformed stages. The term transformation is closely related to that of function and relation. If we have transformation, we have function and a relation. If we have a function, we have a relation and a transformation. If we have a relation, we have a function and a transformation.

While mathematics is not a very superior activity of the human mind, it is perhaps the easiest or simplest activity, and has been able to produce a structurally complete product of the simple kind. The structure of mathematics, because of this oversimplicity yet structural similarity with the external world, makes it possible to build verbal systems of remarkable validity. However, physical or daily abstractions differ considerably from mathematical abstractions. In general, physical abstractors, including daily abstractions, are such that particulars are left out. In other words, no description or definition will ever include everything or all particulars. Mathematics represents a fictitious and oversimplified verbal world. It appears as a language of the highest perfection but has limitations as far as development. Our other language would appear as the other extreme. There exists a structural gap between the two languages. The bridging of the gap is necessary if we are to understand *adequate*, as well as *accurate*, correspondence. The processes of abstracting are designed to bring ordinary "language" closer to mathematics, and mathematics closer to ordinary languages. When that occurs, mathematics as we know it may become obsolete, but only if we identify the epistemology behind the math. Now, we move back to the unspeakable that produced the mathematics.

If we are going to create structural similarity, theoretically and linguistically, that represents somewhat the event with "classifications" that match, where do we focus? If we begin with the assumption that we have made progress with the language of mathematics and the nervous system, and those mathematical notions are undergirded by or simultaneously emerged with transformation, invariance, relation and function, it stands to reason (without resorting to the chicken and the egg equation) that we should focus on the language, and/or process which produced this mathematical correspondence. Our job then is to internalize those processes (the language and/or process that produced the mathematical correspondence) and thus, automatically, our functions, creations, and inventions, plus classifications, will have a structural similarity. That correspondence emerges from an internalized equation that has as its focus the nervous system and the natural functioning of same.

My research indicates that the inventors of these accurate systems, or equations, were and are those who have a romance with the notions of transformation, emergence, evolving, invariance, probability,

New Thinking For A New Millennium

postulation, relation, function, and so on. These notions have meaning to the inventors and can be referred to something concrete. They move from theory to application, but unlike the distinction made theoretically and analytically between theoretical and applied mathematics, the theory and application are theoretical-analytical, one process.

If mathematics is the correct language, and we pinpoint how mathematics came about, then we create a deeper insight of correspondence. It stands to reason that if we invent and innovate through the language of mathematics, we ought to seek an understanding, to some extent, from the epistemological undergirding process. That undergirding process takes the form of conceptual notions that can be understood. Therefore, on a deeper level, our thinking has to be about the process that brought about the undergirding process of mathematics. Simply stated vertically, this would take the form of looking at a process that brought about the math, and the undergirding process behind that process. From the standpoint of circularity, it would be sufficient just to focus on the mathematics and the undergirding process as proper, since these two appear to produce each other. However, it would be foolhardy to stop there, since we are entering a time of quarks and black holes. We want to penetrate the very vitals of the processes that transcend mathematics and those mysterious places that give rise to the mathematical undergirding processes in the first place. Therefore, we must look vertically and horizontally and use circularity. A language that enables us to do this may be found in what we already know.

The consistent success of mathematics as a description of the workings of realities and the ability of the human mind to discover and invent mathematical truths appear to be due, to some extent, to the notion of abstracting. The question we must pose, however, is, "How did we come up with the notion of abstracting and the idea that abstracting is the key to providing notions about the notion of abstracting?" The notion of abstracting as a key term is itself the labeling of a process. Before the labeling, what happened? Difficult question? Yes! Impossible? No! The question has to be asked differently. It is not the why of abstracting (this would speak to final causes), but we must ask, "How did it [abstracting] occur?" The answer is: history and the natural circularity of the brain. The human "mind" appears to be constructed in such a way that it naturally grasps some synthetic a priori aspects of the world. Our minds naturally sift out certain aspects of reality. Combining the brain with analytical history, evolving enables us to connect with the synthetic emergings. The historical notion of abstracting evolved out of this process. Our minds have been honed toward their present state by a perpetual process of natural circularity. Due to the natural circularity of the brain, we are able to think about our thinking.

The key term here is circularity. History of evolution and the brain combine to produce correspondence. Thus $c = (f)b + h$ likewise $b + h = (f)c$ (circularity = function of brain and history, likewise brain + history = function of circularity).

This analytical circular process matches the circular process of the brain. To develop intellectual sophistication along with the equation, an in-depth knowledge of ions, nucleons, quarks, quantum physics, black holes, mathematical elegance, proton, neutron, electron, particle physics, and super strings would have to be part of our search. However, a sophisticated knowledge of all of them is not necessary for an understanding and an implementation of correspondence on either the secondary or primary "levels." It simply requires internalizing the processes of abstracting and the implications. Correspondence emerges out of this usage.

This brings us to the chapters that describe these processes. Chapters five, six, and seven are designed to provide us with materials that would enable us to think more deeply about our thinking, provide us with the ability to be more explicit and comprehensive, and, perhaps in the final analysis, allow us to become more adept at primary correspondence.

In summary, there are two aspects to the notion of correspondence. One has to do with naming a "new" phenomenon with a new name (primary). This requires invention. The other is about renaming a phenomenon that has already been named (secondary). In both instances, a similar process is used. Let's take the notion of *interaction* that was replaced by Bentley in *Knowing and the Known* with the label of "*transaction.*" Bentley selected this name after conceptualizing activities that take place when individuals, organizations, institutions, and the like come together. He concluded, based on the history of human development and knowledge of the human condition, that the label interact was inappropriate for understanding the configuration of processes that take place between humans with themselves, others, institutions, and systems. Bentley probably based this invention on what was introduced earlier with the invention of relativity and quantum mechanics. Bentley realized that the notion of interaction represented

New Thinking For A New Millennium

"old thinking." It is mechanical and describes more of a static world. Transaction, on the other hand, describes dynamic motion and process. Interaction spoke to separate, non-process, static, thinking and human processes being "still" until moved by an outside force. The new thinking is about things being together and in motion at all times, a departure from fixed thinking. Therefore, a new naming was needed to convey this innovative discovery in thinking, and consequently, the notion of transaction. Let us now see how this works out in everyday affairs and our common sense world. In other words, what does a "busy" person do? Since most of us are not immersed in primary knowledge, to function with ease in making our analyses, evaluations, and "sound" decisions, we need to hold as constant two fundamentals. One is the policy of nonfragmentation, and the other is nonelementalism. They both mean nonseparation of entities. For example, instead of space and time, space-time, and instead of mind and emotions, mind-emotions.

On a more sophisticated order of abstraction, we need to be conscious of the processes of abstracting. For example, in types of abstracting we find that the fourth type automatically rejects fragmentation and elementalism, and introduces the principle of postulation. The history we spoke about earlier is automatically built into the abstracting processes, especially types of abstracting. We find that by using types we are able to identify certain namings and categories. For example, we know that the fourth type dictates that we use the notion of transaction, rather than interaction, since interaction is in the third type. We also know that the third type leads to fragmentation, elementalism, and the process of interaction. By using this process, we can automatically decide what certain labels mean. The information is already designed for us and we know what to call something, but what do we do when a new label or naming is not given? Suppose for example, we decide that the "concepts" of leadership, motivation, conflict, decision-making, and so on, are not appropriate any longer because they are fragmented and elementalistic. Is it necessary to find new namings, categories, or labels? The answer is no, and for two reasons: (1) the moment we move to type four abstracting, we no longer label; and (2) the new outlook speaks to a wholeness and nonfragmentation. We know then that the underlying epistemological process of transaction is sufficient. We no longer refer to the processes as singular. We, in our qualitative analysis, see a process meshing and functioning without labeling the behaviors, thus forcing ourselves to become more descriptive of what is taking place. Our first order abstraction (description) will embrace all of the elements we once saw as pieces; that is, leadership, motivation, conflict, and so on. They become one and we know there is some of each in every transaction. Our interpretation will then focus on the situation and the processes, rendering the terms motivation, leadership, and conflict obsolete. These terms are not descriptions. They are high-order abstractions and "buzzwords." The notion of transaction is a piece in the puzzle of the interconnectedness of things.

If we must call it something, it ought to be a phrase that unifies these nonreferential concepts. Simultaneously, old definitions must be rejected, and we are no longer evaluating something called leadership, but transactions in process.

The processes described in this book will lead us in this direction. The internalizing of these processes, or just some of them, will supply us with the flexibility needed. Essentially, we are about having our thinking process correspond with the event taking place. We raised the question of how do we know when that thinking is in correspondence. We know by using the formulation embracing the abstracting processes. We have come full circle.

In the case of those dealing primarily with secondary matters, the adoption of nonfragmentation and nonelementalism alone can provide powerful results. Once we include into the equation the inquiry methods of the processes of abstracting, the epistemological profile, and, generally, the *abduction* perspective, we move vigorously into the direction of accurate and adequate correspondence.

In the final analysis, I cannot overemphasize the necessity for a shift in thinking and language in order to bring about correspondence both on secondary and primary "levels." That is exactly what mathematicians do. They take leave of the common sense ways of thinking and expression. Moving from the common sense way of thinking is childishly simple and thus is one of the difficulties adults encounter.

A Conclusion

"We know a great deal about linear math. In comparison, we know almost nothing about nonlinear math except that almost all math is nonlinear," according to Kosko in *Fuzzy Thinking,* page 108. "So it is a good bet that some day quantum mechanics will fall because it is linear to its core" (Kosko 1993). My interpretation of this is that the author means that, theoretically, most math and nature are nonlinear; but too often our application of them is linear. The key term here is application.

Heisenberg advocated in quantum mechanics that there are some things we can never know; they are unknowable in principle. He made doubt scientific, meaning that it became concrete, solid, and irrefutable. At the time probability theory was the only way known to put this doubt in math form. So, rather than shift us from black-white truth to gray truth, the uncertainty principle had the effect of shifting to the probability of all-or-nonbivalent truth. Probability theory says that it will later be something we know or cannot know, and thus, probably one or the other, but definitely one (Kosko 1993). These simple probability models may fail to capture the nonlinear world. Much of the nonlinear math is not describable in terms of binary concepts and probability distributions.

However, probabilists feel that there was no difference between the *Fuzzy* principles and their principles. They said the new nonlinear theory that eschewed uncertainty and probability, which the multivalued proponents call vagueness, was randomness used in disguise.

These disagreements may enable us to point to something specific, or where we should focus. If I take the processes of abstracting and analyze these differing positions, I find that levels of abstracting and the notion of multiordinality provide some clarity. For example, the notions of linear and nonlinear are not opposites. They are different types of abstracting and are on different levels of abstracting.

Therefore, it is not a matter of choosing between one or the other, but a matter of finding how and when each should be used. The same applies to uncertainty and probability. They are multiordinal terms that have different meanings at different levels of abstracting. With all— linear, nonlinear, uncertainty, and probability—when we involve types of abstracting we get different meanings and different definitions with different types and stages. There is a horizontal assumption built into the argument about linearity versus nonlinearity and nonprobability versus probability. If we view these descriptions as vertical, we easily see that at different levels, as we go up and down, all of these notions mean different things at the different levels and therefore have usage and usefulness in differing contexts.

Our focus then, in qualitative analysis and proper correspondence, is not about inventing new math but inventing processes that brought about the math. That process has to do with a constant application of the processes of abstracting and simultaneously inventing new forms in keeping with that process. The latter should emerge with the mere usage of the formulation, which automatically moves us beyond quibbling about what we call something to how we see connections. This is about thinking about our thinking. It is a focus on the "secrets of the universe," an attempt to constantly engage the search for some deeper principle from which all other knowledge flows. The key terms here are constantly engage and search, because finding would be absolute. It may be just a process.

Chapter Three

The Verb "To Be:" Fundamental Focus—
The Use of

Abstracting, as qualitative analysis, engages the limitations of the verb "to be." One answer to the difficulties surrounding the verb "to be" has been the introduction of E-prime. The term E-prime refers to a proposed process designed to eliminate the use of the verb "to be" in any form (such as "am," "is," "are," "was," "were," "be," and "been"). Dr. Albert Ellis, in his book *A New Guide to Rational Living,* utilized the theory of *nonidentity,* which eliminates the *is of identity.* The contention is: our grammar in embracing "is" doesn't offer adequacy in information. The verb encourages final causes, giving us a static picture of the world and an ultimate representation of Aristotelian logic. The use of E-prime, in practice, moves one beyond a two-valued, either/or, Aristotelian orientation, which describes the world in simplistic terms, such as true or false, black or white, or all or none (International Society for General Semantics 1991).

Difficulties that "are" unsolvable in ordinary English sometimes appear solvable in E-prime. "This subtle shift in attitude can make a great difference" (International Society for General Semantics 1991). When we use E-prime, we eliminate the degree of finality implied in the verb "to be." Ultimately, part of the mind continues working on the difficulty and often finds one or more solutions to it.

"E-prime fosters a world view in which the user perceives situations as changeable, rather than static, and where verbal statements derived from experience indicate possibilities rather than certainties" (International Society for General Semantics 1987). In the book *Language, Thought and Reality,* Benjamin Lee Whorf is credited with giving us numerous examples of languages and cultures that support his "principle of linguistic relativity." The principle states that the structure of the language one uses influences the way one perceives "reality," as

New Thinking For A New Millennium

well as how one behaves with respect to that perceived reality. E-prime has the purpose of producing a language structure that is designed to implement Whorf's perspective. Optimally, it would include other linguistic devices, such as dating and indexing. E-prime substitutes for forms of "to be" with: seems, appears, feels, acts, or looks. The elimination of the "is" of identity makes the use of subject-predicate language impossible, forcing us to use verbs that produce action in straightforward statements. E-prime encourages one to use the active voice (he did it), rather than the passive voice (it was done).

Any meticulous, rigorous analysis should deal with the verb "to be." In his book *Science and Sanity,* Korzybski referred to these difficulties as the *is of predication* and the *is of identity*. In both, he blamed the *verb to be* for misleading people into making untrue and unwarranted assumptions. We do not realize how much everything changes, because the *verb to be* gives an illusion of permanence, preventing us from recognizing when change occurs. Our language remains the language of absolutes, and the reason, to a large extent, is with the *verb to be*. The spurious identity it fosters perverts our perception of realities. Our focus should shape as follows for meticulous analysis: subject-linking–verb-adjective reveals an is of predication, and the subject-linking–verb-noun patterns the is of identity. In other words, every time we use "is," to varying degrees, we restrict, distort, lie, and lull ourselves into mistaken judgment. How does this occur? In the instance of the is of predication, we would look for something like this: Bill is absent. The verb links or couples the subject to the predicate adjective to note a fact. This is probably all right. Bill is stupid. The same grammatical structure inheres, but does not provide a verifiable report. There is only the opinion of an agent who hides outside the statement. In both cases, the *verb to be* indiscriminately relates the subject and the predicate, implying that they equal one another. As we do our analysis, we distinguish between these structures that happen to look the same, but give different results. In this case, one is a proposition (Bill is absent), and the other is a propositional function (Bill is stupid). In other words, our analysis includes the necessity for discriminating between one kind of subject-linking–verb-predicate adjective and another, although they both fall under the general heading of the *is of predication*.

The subject-linking–verb-noun should also be meticulously analyzed. For example, Mr. Jones is my director and Mr. Jones is a space cadet. Both have the same grammatical structure but provide

Dr. William J. Williams

different results. Again, as in the *is of predication*, we distinguish between the factual and the harmless, and the nonfactual and the harmful. The former is factual and harmless, while the latter is nonfactual and harmful.

In both instances of the *is of predication* and the *is of identity* (the harmless and the harmful), we are saddled with statements that pigeonhole. Both limit, in a similar manner, our ability to perceive Bill and Mr. Jones as whole persons.

The *verb to be* provides the epistemological underpinning. To overcome the *verb to be*, the following principles ought to be introduced: nonidentity, nonallness, and self-reflexiveness. Two additional laws hide in the absoluteness of the *verb to be*, the laws of commandment and permanency—and the antidotes are process and nonabsoluteness.

The focus on the *verb to be* as part of rigorous, meticulous analysis can determine, in substantive terms, the *orders* of abstraction, pinpoint *levels*, and give some indication of the *type* of abstracting. In the example of Mr. Jones is director, this is the factual part of the subject-linking–verb–noun. In terms of orders of abstraction, where would this fit? Would it be the event, first-order experience, description, or statement? It is certainly not the event, nor is it a first-order experience, and it falls short of a description. Though factual, it is a statement or label. It turns out to be a propositional function. As we noted earlier, the *verb to be* (the is of predication) inheres in this statement. An application of levels of abstracting places the statement at the classifying *level* of abstracting and, particularly at the objective step. At this point the statement becomes a proposition. What does all of this mean? This rigorous, qualitative analysis enables us to determine the value of the statement. Determining where it resides prevents us from confusing *levels* and *types* of abstracting. This will be explained in the section on implementation.

Is *E-prime* the answer to this difficulty? E-prime is ponderous, time-consuming, and difficult to implement. Therefore, for practical purposes, I recommend *E-choice*, which simply means that we just become aware of the different ways that "is" is used; that is, what *level*, *order*, and *type* of abstracting may be involved. In short, I recommend still using *is* with the idea of explaining with adequacy the *order*, *level*, and *type* of abstracting. As in this instance I use is to talk about *is*. This is *E-choice*. It is inappropriate in terms of E-prime, because E-prime is on the side of purity. The processes of abstracting which enabled us in the first place to identify *is* as inappropriate also enables us to determine when "is" is harmful and when *is* does not lead to harmful consequences.

E-prime, in my judgment, gives us a mechanical way of meeting the difficulty presented by the *is of identity*. The usage of the processes of abstracting, however, provides us with a formulation that is nonmechanical and eliminates the difficulty inherent in the *is of identity* automatically.

Why then would I devote space to E-prime? Space is given to E-prime because of its mechanical value as a dissecting part of the overall application of the processes of abstracting. For example, when we use *types* and *levels* to determine where a particular statement fits, the criteria of E-prime enables us to communicate in explicit terms how we made our judgment.

Chapter Four

Epistemological Background for Knowing and Naming

Any full discussion or rigorous, meticulous, qualitative analysis has to include, if it is to be meticulous, something on the origins and emergence of views, tools, and language for the selection of new symbols.

In the first instance, an evaluation of the present symbols, ideas, and language being used is automatically done with "types" of abstracting. However, the criteria for choosing new constructs and formulations to supplant them or present innovative ideas resides specifically in a kind of perspective (worldview and mindset) and an epistemological method.

The following will clarify, to some extent, how to view the present symbols and develop new symbols and formulations.

Epistemological Perspective for Knowing and Naming

Art, science, and human work, in general, are divided up into specialties, each considered to be separate from the other. Becoming dissatisfied with the state of affairs, we set up interdisciplinary subjects intended to unite specialties, but we end up creating separate fragments. Society as a whole has in the same way broken up into separate nations and religious, political, economic, social, and racial groups. The natural environment has thus been seen as an aggregate of separate, existent parts. Each human being has been fragmented into a large number of separate and conflicting compartments. It has always been both necessary and proper for humans to divide things up and separate them into parts. In certain ways, the creation of special subjects of study and division of labor was an important step forward. It enabled us to reduce our difficulties to manageable proportions. Nevertheless, the ability to separate the environment from ourselves, and to divide and apportion things, led to a wide range of negative and destructive results. We extended the process of division beyond the limits within which it works properly. The process of division is a way of thinking about things useful mainly in the domain of teaching and mechanical logical "common sense" activities; for example, dividing up a piece of land, building an engine, and assigning people to areas of work. When this mode of thinking is applied more broadly to parts of ourselves and the whole world in which we live (worldview), the divisions are not useful or convenient tools. Guided by a fragmentary self-worldview, we act and break up the world according to our thinking. The fragmentation we create takes on an autonomous existence.

There appears to be two different lines of operation. For example, the word health in English is based on an Anglo-Saxon word "hole" meaning "whole." To be healthy is to be whole, which is equivalent to the Hebrew "shalom." Likewise, the English "holy" is based on the same root as "whole." This suggests that humans have sensed that wholeness is an absolute necessity. However, we have generally lived in fragmentation. Since our thought is pervaded with differences and distinctions, it follows that such a habit leads us to look on these as real divisions, so that the world is then seen and experienced as actually broken up into fragments.

The relationship between thought and reality is in fact far more complex than that of a mere correspondence. It is about theory. Thus, in scientific research, a great deal of our thinking is in terms of theories. The word "theory" is derived from the Greek "theoria," which has the same root as "theater," in a word meaning "to view" or "to make a spectacle." Thus, it might be said that a theory is primarily a form of insight; that is, a way of looking at the world, and not a form of knowledge of how the world is.

In ancient times, men had a theory that celestial matter was fundamentally different from earthly matter. The theory was that it was natural for earthly objects to fall and for celestial objects, such as the moon, to remain up in the sky. In a sudden flash of insight, Newton saw that as the apple falls, so does the moon, and so indeed do all objects. Thus, he invented the theory of universal gravitation, in which all objects were seen as falling toward various centers (e.g. the earth, the sun, and the planets). This constituted a new way of looking at the heavens in which the movements of the planets were no longer seen through the ancient notion of an essential difference between heavenly and earthly matter.

Dr. William J. Williams

The Newtonian form of insight worked very well for several centuries, but ultimately, like the ancient Greek insights that came before, it led to unclear results when extended into new domains. In these new domains, new forms of insight were developed (the theory of relativity and the quantum theory). These gave a radically different picture of the world from that of Newton, although the latter was, of course, found to be still valid in a limited domain. If we supposed that theories give true knowledge, corresponding to reality as it is, then we would have to conclude that Newtonian theory was true until around 1900, after which it suddenly became false, while relativity and quantum theory suddenly became the truth. Such an absurd conclusion does not arise. However, we may say that all theories are insights, which are neither true nor false but represent what we know at the present time. Therefore, instead of supposing that older theories are falsified at a certain point in time, we merely say that we are continually developing new forms of insight based on what we know at that time. In this activity, there is evidently no reason to suppose that there is or will be a final form of insight corresponding to absolute truth.

When we look at the world through our theoretical insights, the factual knowledge that we obtain will evidently be shaped and formed by our theories. For example, in ancient times, the fact about the motion of the planets was described in terms of the Ptolemaic idea of epicycles (circles on top of circles). In Newton's time, this fact was described in terms of planetary orbits and analyzed through rates of objects falling toward various centers. Later came relativity, Einstein's concepts of space and time. Still later, a very different sort of fact was specified in terms of the quantum theory, which gives in general only a statistical fact. In biology, the fact is now described in terms of the theory of evolution, but in earlier times it was expressed in terms of fixed species of living beings.

As has been first pointed out by ants, all experience is organized according to the categories of our thought; that is, our ways of thinking about space, time, matter, substance, causality, contingency, necessity, universality, and particularity. It can be said that these categories are general forms of insight, or ways of looking at everything, so that in a certain sense they are a kind of theory.

We sometimes are unaware that our theories are ever-changing forms of insight giving shape and form to experience, in general, and yet may be vision-limiting. One could put it like this: experience with nature is very much like experience with human beings. If one

New Thinking For A New Millennium

approaches another person with a fixed "theory" that the person is an enemy against whom one must defend, the person may respond similarly, and thus one's "theory" will be apparently confirmed by experience. Similarly, nature appears to respond in accordance with the theory with which it is approached.

What prevents theoretical insight from going beyond existing limitations and changing to meet new facts is just the belief that theories give true knowledge of reality, which implies that they need never change.

If we regard theories as "direct descriptions of reality as it is," then we will inevitably treat these differences and distinctions as divisions, implying separate existence of the various elementary terms appearing in the theory. Therefore, we will be led to the illusion that the world is actually constituted of separate fragments. This will cause us to act in such a way that we do, in fact, produce the very fragmentation implied in our attitude to the theory.

One can no longer maintain the division between the observer and the observed, which is implicit in the atomistic view. One has to view the world in terms of a universal flux of events and processes.

We can however, in specified contexts, adopt other forms of insight that enables us to simplify certain things, to treat them momentarily and, for certain limited purposes, as if they were autonomous and stable as well as perhaps separately existent. Yet we do not have to fall into the trap of looking at ourselves, in general, in this way. Our thoughts must reject the illusion that reality is actually of fragmentary nature.

One may be puzzled by a wide range of factors of things that do not fit together, until suddenly there is a flash of understanding, and, thereafter, one sees how all of these factors are related as aspects of one totality; for example, consider Newton's insight into universal gravitation. Such acts of perception cannot properly be given a detailed analysis or description. Rather, they are to be considered as aspects of the forming activity of the mind. A particular structure or formulation is then the product of this activity.

Fragmentary perception is a largely unconscious habit of confusion around the question of what is different and what is not. Therefore, in the very act in which we try to discover what to do about fragmentation, we will go on with this habit and thus will tend to introduce yet further forms of fragmentation.

This does not necessarily mean, of course, that there is no way out at all. However, it does mean that we have to give pause, so that we do

Dr. William J. Williams

not go on with our habitual fragmentary ways of thinking as we seek solutions that are already at hand. The question of fragmentation and wholeness is a subtle and difficult one— more subtle and difficult than those that lead to fundamentally new discoveries in science. To ask how to end fragmentation and to expect an answer in a few minutes makes even less sense than asking how to develop a theory as new as Einstein's was when he was working on it.

What we have to deal with here is a oneness of the thinking process and its content, similar in key ways to the oneness of observer and observed that has been discussed in connection with relativity theory and quantum theory. Questions of this nature cannot be met properly while we are caught up, consciously or unconsciously, in a mode of thought which attempts to analyze itself in terms of a presumed separation between the process of thinking and the content of thought. We are ready to give such attention and work in a wide range of fields— scientific, economic, social, and political. As of yet, however, little or none of this has gone into the creation of insight into the process of thought, on which all else depends. What is primarily needed is a growing realization of the extreme danger of going on with a fragmentary process of thought. Such a realization would give the inquiry into how thought actually operates and the sense of urgency and energy required to meet the true magnitude of the difficulties with which fragmentation is now confronting us.

What should be said is that wholeness is real, and that fragmentation is the response with the fragmentary approach. In other words, we will inevitably be answered with a correspondingly fragmentary response. What is needed for us to give attention to this habit of fragmentary thought, to be aware of it, and thus to bring it to an end? Our approach to reality may then be whole, and therefore the response will be whole. However, for this to happen, it is crucial that we be aware of the activity of our thoughts; that is, as a form of insight and a way of looking rather than as a "true copy of reality as it is."

What is called for is not an integration of thought or a kind of imposed unity, for any such imposed point of view would itself be merely another fragment. Rather, all of our different ways of thinking are to be considered as different ways of looking at the one reality, each with some domain in which it is clear and adequate. To a considerable extent, it is in these worldviews that our general notions of the nature of reality, and of the relationship between our thought and reality, are implicitly or explicitly formed. One can obtain some insights into this

New Thinking For A New Millennium

way of thinking by considering the earlier meanings of certain words. Thus, the Latin "mederi," meaning "to cure" (the root of the modern "medicine"), is based on a root meaning "to measure." This reflects the view that physical health is to be regarded as the outcome of a state of right inward measure in all arts and processes of the body. Similarly, the word "moderation," which describes one of the prime ancient notions of virtue, is based on the same root, and this shows that such virtue has been regarded as the outcome of right inner measure underlining our social actions and behavior. Again, the word "mediation," which is based on the same root, implies a kind of weighing, pondering, or measuring of the whole process of thought, which could bring the inner activities of the mind to a state of harmonious measure. Therefore, physically, socially, and mentally, awareness of the inner measure of things has been seen as the essential key to a healthy, happy, harmonious life.

It is useful to call to mind ancient Greek notions of measure in music and in the visual arts. These notions emphasized that a grasp of measure was a key to the understanding of harmony in music; that is, measure as rhythm, right proportion in intensity of sound, and right proportion in totality. Likewise, in the visual arts, right measure was seen as essential to overall harmony and beauty; for example consider the "golden mean." All of this indicates how far the notion of measure went beyond that of comparison, with an external standard, to point to a universal sort of inner ratio or proportion perceived both through the senses and through the mind.

Yet, of course, as time went on, this notion of measure gradually began to change, lose its subtlety, and become relatively gross and mechanical. The general rigidification and objectification of the notion of measure continued to develop, until in modern times the very word "measure" came to denote mainly a process of comparison of something with an external standard. While the original meaning still survives in some contexts (e.g. art and mathematics), it is generally felt to have only a secondary sort of significance.

Now, in the East, the notion of measure has not played nearly as fundamental a role. Rather, in the prevailing philosophy of the Orient, the immeasurable—that which cannot be named, described, or understood through any form of reason—is regarded as the primary reality. It is clear that the different ways the two societies have developed fits in with their different attitudes to measure. Thus, in the West, society has mainly emphasized the development of science and

Dr. William J. Williams

technology (dependent on measure), while in the East, the main emphasis has gone to religion and philosophy (directed ultimately toward the immeasurable).

It is, of course, impossible to go back to a state of wholeness that may have been present before the split between East and West developed—only because we know little, if anything, about this state. Rather, what is needed is to learn afresh, to observe, and to discover for ourselves the meaning of wholeness. Of course, we have to be cognizant of the teachings of the past, both Western and Eastern. Yet, to imitate these teachings or to try to conform to them would have little value. To develop new insight into fragmentation and wholeness requires a creative work, even more difficult than that which is needed to make fundamental new discoveries in science, or to create great and original works of art. Fragmentation originates in the fixing of the insights forming our overall self-worldview, which is based on our generally mechanical, routinized, and habitual modes of thought about these matters. Because the primary reality goes beyond anything that can be contained in such fixed forms of measure, these insights eventually cease to be adequate and give rise to various forms of unclarity or confusion. However, when the whole field of measure becomes open to original and creative insight without any fixed limits or barriers, our overall world views will cease to be rigid, and the whole field of measure will come into harmony as fragmentation comes to an end. The measurable and the immeasurable will then be in harmony, and indeed one will see that they are but different ways of considering the one and undivided whole.

When such harmony prevails, we can then not only have insight into the meaning of wholeness, but we can realize the truth of this insight in every phase and aspect of our lives. Much of the information from the previous page was prompted by a reading of David Bohm's *Fragmentation and Wholeness*.

We now turn to a method for pursuing and implementing the nonfragmentation perspective. I will introduce and formulate some qualitative methods. They are: (1) root metaphors, by Stephen Pepper, (2) mental models, by Kenneth Boulding, (3) epistemological profile, by Gaston Bachelard and J. Samuel Bois, and (4) the conceptual revolutions, by Percy Bridgeman.

Many of the elements from each of the above will be integrated under the rubric of Pepper's root metaphors. Since only the *epistemological profile* deals with the time before the intrusion of

New Thinking For A New Millennium

Aristotelian logic, I will begin with a stage from the epistemological profile, which has no counterpart in any of the other methods. It will enable us to complete our nonfragmenting methodological process. By including stage one of the profile, we will end up with a formulation of five discrete conceptual notions. The first is *primitive realism*, or the *sensing stage* of the profile. This stage is characterized by unquestioned identification. Man's perception is the measure of things and of their qualities. The is of identity is taken as the adequate formulation of what is going on. Subjective experience (total organismic semantic reaction) goes unchecked and unanalyzed. It is taken as the relation and the measure of the event. There is a low degree of conditionality. There are signal reactions—a "copying" of animals, or a non-consciousness of abstracting. Whatever abstracting takes place is animistic, mythological, or purely verbal-reifying (projective). Mathematics is limited to the sensing: "one, two, three . . . infinity," an unsophisticated semantic reaction to what happens labeled with the traditionally accepted term, without any critical examination of either the event or the term. The event is what the term says it is. Classifications in terms of subjective values, which are often imposed by the cultural environment, are not reexamined, questioned, or doubted.

Simple experiments show that there are, in most of us, remnants of primitive semantic reactions. If you mention the sucking of a lemon, my mouth waters. If I lift three cans of equal weight and different sizes, I feel that the biggest is the heaviest. I can't bring myself to cut the eyes of my mother in a photo. The water is cold because I feel it is cold. Pancakes cause indigestion because they once gave me indigestion. This stage represents an era before we officially conceptualized and classified. It is pre-Aristotelian. The key term here is *reactive*.

Now, we move to the four areas represented by the root metaphors. They are *formism, mechanism, organicism,* and *contextualism*. We begin with the root metaphors and include the elements from the other qualitative methods, along with the key ideas and terms to be emphasized.

The first root metaphor is formism: (a) framework, (b) inanimate or nonmoving, (c) description or static structure (container, receptacle, clean slate), (d) classificatory, (e) hierarchical, (f) enumeration of parts, (g) reflector rather than projector, (h) static model; diagram, map, or chart (description of function, but not functioning), and (i) simple common sense notions (things that seem to be just like blades of grass, leaves on a tree, or a set of spoons). It is no more than a systemization

Dr. William J. Williams

of the categorical distinctions in formism between relations and ties: a positivistic view (the world of the observed and the observer)—either/or thinking, fixed, classifications, static, and passive. The framework (suitable for relatively permanent things such as roads, towns, continents, or living organisms— dissected into anatomical parts). (early Greek thinking 650–350 B.C.).

Key notions are Aristotelian logic (syllogistic reasoning), deduction (macroscopic), analysis categorizing, and subject-predicate language. Key terms are essence, structure, hierarchy balance, monuments, substance, symmetry, permanence, space, addition, consistency, and observer.

Emphasis is on common-sense perception of similar things. The world is full of things that seem to be just alike and, yet, with more careful scrutiny, we find they are not exactly alike. Things and people who operate as if they are both alike and the same are formistic thinkers. The metaphor describing the human mind as a blank slate or the creative imagination as a mirror would be a variation of the formistic framework model. Literal metaphors would compare human beings to clocks, rocks, or pieces of chalk. The image of a framework model would be that of a solid, permanent object; for example, a mountain, town, or continent. Living things on the framework level can only identify anatomical parts of an organism but not its functioning. A framework system model can contain a statement of the constituent parts but not a description of the functioning. For example, diagrams and schemes in textbooks, without special symbols to denote movement, are of the framework static variety. Organizational charts, blueprints of the climate that produced the formistic framework model, began with the classical philosophers Plato and Aristotle, who sought to find the real nature of things. Aristotelian philosophy tends to be relatively static, elementalistic, and bound up in concepts, such as substance and quality. The root metaphor for the framework or formistic model can be traced to Aristotle and Plato. The framework-formistic model was considered to be an accurate image of the mind during the time of John Locke, who conceived of the mind as a blank slate. The static image, until the era of Newtonian dynamics, remained the dominant root metaphor. Some might remember the hearing during the confirmation of Clarence Thomas for Supreme Court justiceship. He said, and I quote, "I arrive with a blank mind, a clean slate, an empty vessel when I approach a subject," shades of Aristotle. Justice Thomas is formistic, static, and mentally in 650 B.C. His thinking is obsolete. The characteristics of the

New Thinking For A New Millennium

formistic framework model are static rather than dynamic, passive rather than active, reactive rather than active, descriptive of the function but not functioning and not moving.

The second root metaphor is mechanism: (a) clockwork model, (b) dynamic moving structure, (c) interdependent activity, (d) repeating property, (e) empowered from outside, (f) Cyclical regularity, (g) symbolized by flowchart models, (h) thermostat model (self-regulation, homeostatic), (i) reacts to feedback, (j) opposite to opposite principle, (k) self-monitoring, (l) self-controlling, (m) digital computer analogue (binary function).

Clockwork structure: The key term is interaction. The clockwork model is suitable for a machine and interdependent active parts. The notion of flowcharting grew out of this model. It is like the thermostat with built-in controls for adjusting inaccuracies. This self-regulating feature was made necessary by advances in the science of cybernetics and the self-correcting computer. If man's world was seen only in terms of "human engineering," this model probably would have been sufficient.

The root metaphor of mechanism is a machine. A recent revolution in physics consisted largely in a shift from what is called a mechanical theory of matter to an electrical theory. This is a shift from lever to electromagnetic field. Many details are altered by this shift, but since the basic categories are the same, the general theoretical attitude is not changed. The term mechanism, however, which we are using for this type of world theory, must not be identified with the mechanical theory of matter. The shift from lever to electromagnetic field was not trifling. Therefore, certain mechanical processes, such as field theory, relativity, and quantum, will fit more readily under contextualism. This mechanism is about push and pull physics and Newtonian character, and it resides in the seventeenth-century format. When independent moving parts are added to the framework- formistic model, the root metaphor is shifted dramatically from formism to mechanism. An abstract for this mental model might be dynamic structure. Each axle, cog, or gear must contribute to the workings of the whole unit.

Key notions are action-reaction, cause and effect, checks and balances, and induction. Key terms are action, dynamic, function, interaction, causality, smooth running, asymmetry, entropy, space and time, multiplication, manipulation, doing, self-improvement, envy, machines, mathematics, determinism.

Dr. William J. Williams

Emphasis is on the origins of the mechanism and clockwork metaphors, which go back to the second century. The components are the wheel and the balance. The wheel itself is an old, useful archetype which has been translated with "wheel of fortune" and "wheel of fate." It is mainly the age of Newton and Sir Francis Bacon. The concept eventually emerged in the works of the eighteenth-century Deist, who envisioned God as a cosmic clockmaker who wound up the universe and set it running according to predictable, controllable laws. Locke was instrumental in developing the mechanistic metaphor, with the "checks and balances" concept appearing in the *Two Treatises of Government*. The football or basketball coach who insists that each member work as part of a well-timed machine, as well as the drill sergeant who likes his troops to function as a machine, have internalized the image of the smooth-running, interdependent machine. The American system of checks and balances imaged in the Constitution emerged out of this kind of thinking. The circulatory system, the autonomic nervous system, the reproductive system, and the digestive system, when healthy, function with clocklike regularity. The resemblance of the human being to the clock led Julien Offray de La Mettrie to entitle his book *Man a Machine,* and Descartes to regard l'homme Machine. David Hume, nearly a century after Descartes, describes all of nature in terms of a gigantic clockwork or mechanistic metaphor.

With the clockwork model, foreign policy is prevented from returning to the more primitive framework concept of isolationism. Dependency or interdependency leads each nation to consider itself not as a self-contained entity, but as a functional subunit of a global effort. Journalists are replete with terms, such as the ill-timed move and miscalculation when the American president evaluates a new economic policy. The pros and cons are carefully weighed, keeping a proper balance and perspective.

Psychologists who subscribe to the stimulus-response model are fixated at the clockwork level of metaphoric maturity. The flowcharts of economics illustrating the multiplier theory are examples of theoretical constructs at the clockwork level. Matthew Arnold's vehicle of the ebb and flow of the sea as a model of the life process reflects the clockwork mental model. Seasonal cycles, weather patterns, and interdependent systems of the human body can be explained by means of a mechanical clockwork analogy. This mechanism model is a progression from the clockwork to the homeostatic modes. Heat with engines, described by analogy from thermodynamics, displaced the old mechanism of "Newtonian dynamics."

The self-regulating thermostat, however, produced more sophisticated analogues. The science of cybernetics produces self-monitoring, self-controlling, and self-steering, requiring no adjustment once set upon the predetermined course. The abstract concept of feedback is described using this homeostatic analogy. Homeostatic analogies are used to explain the peaks and dips of economic cycles, as well as changes in the political climate.

The root metaphor of the homeostatic thermostat can be traced to the German philosopher Georg Wilhelm Friedrich Hegel in his thesis "Anti-thesis Synthesis and Back to Thesis." Administrators want feedback from subordinates. Teachers and students desire feedback from each other. Elected officials, entertainers, and adventurers are into feedback, both positive and adverse. If one does not care to envision human beings as anything more than robots, guided missiles, or even higher-order computers, mechanical metaphors would suffice to explain the behavior of a human being. However, to discuss more about the human being, we must move beyond framework-form, mechanism clockwork to the biological.

The third root metaphor is organicism: biological cell model, (b) self-maintaining and self-repairing, (c) self-reproducing, (d) ingestion and elimination, (e) plant or tree model, (f) self-expanding, (g) differentiation of function (bark, root, leaves), (h) stable configuration, (i) feeds on and gives back to the environment, (j) seed or fruit bearing, (k) biological animal model, (l) stable animal model, (m) self-moving, and (n) consciousness of self.

What about living organisms? It would be well to look at the biological models. The self-maintaining and self-reproducing structure has all the characteristics of the mechanical models, with the difference that self-maintenance (unlike the clockwork model, which was empowered from the outside) and reproductions are added.

In biological plant models, the self-expanding structure includes all the components of previous models, with the added feature that it repairs damage done to itself, feeds from the environment, and gives back to the environment. In this way, the principle of interaction can be described. This could not have been done with a mechanical model.

In biological animal models, the self-moving structure is not confined to a single spot, such as plants and trees, but can move around seeking more favorable environmental conditions. Bois claims that the

Dr. William J. Williams

animal models "show consciousness of self . . . recognize who is kind to them, and who does not want them around. They are also capable of expressing moods and needs, and can learn by insight."

Organicism, like mechanism, is an integrative mindset. The major difference has organicism as being self-contained and automatic, and the mechanical as dependent, in some cases, on outside forces. The organic believes that every actual event is a more or less concealed, organized process. Therefore, it is more biological. The cell, plant, animal, and humans contain all of the features of previous analogies.

Some key notions are chemistry-binding, space-binding, and time-binding. The plant illustrates the chemistry-binding in its transforming sunlight to chlorophyll through photosynthesis. The animal is able to bind space through its ability to move, such as moving from one location to another. Humans as time-binders show the ability to synthesize past-present-future.

The living cell never at rest until death overtakes it. It is a basic, open system, draws foreign substances from the environment, and does not lose its configuration. There is an emphasis on growth and reproduction, repairing from the inside, interrelatedness, systematization, differentiation, and specialization.

Key terms are organic, evolution, transformation, process-like, emergence, free growth, space-time, development, becoming, complex-ification, participant, transaction, emergence, biota, spiral cycles, and self-renewal.

Organimistic thinking was transplanted from the natural sciences to the social sciences emphasizing the failure of mechanical thinking, with an emphasis on whole evolution, interrelatedness, and growth.

The next image is the plant moving toward a more complex organization. A society of cells, corporation, organization, and plant are direct metaphorical vehicles that business and industry use to describe the nature of their functioning. They incorporate metaphorical vehicles from trees, bushes, shrubs, flowers, and grass. Educators can explain student group concepts—that is, maturing earlier, late bloomers, dormant, unproductive, fruitful, or flowers.

The root metaphor of organicism was brought about by a revolt against the mechanism model from Newtonian and Galilean dynamics. Organimistic methods were introduced into social sciences by Edmund Burke.

The animal analogy, or metaphor, includes movement. The plant model does not. The root metaphor utilizing the animal model can be

New Thinking For A New Millennium

traced to Aristotle who termed man as a rational animal. This was reinforced in 1762, when Jean Jacques Rousseau suggested that a human being at birth is little more than a healthy animal. Charles Darwin continued this by saying that there is no fundamental difference between man and the higher animals. Educational psychologists use the results of animal experimentation to generalize about human behavior. Behaviorists continue to use pigeons, mice, and rats. We are too fixated upon the animal analogue. We see similarities instead of major differences.

Next is the human analogue, which falls more appropriately within the contextual metaphor. The fourth root metaphor is contextualism—human model: (a) thinking; (1) self-reflexive, (2) symbolizing, (3) situation understanding, (4) planning and creating, (5) consciousness of time, (6) capable of overcoming conditioning, and (7) time-binding; (b) feeling (expresses and feels love, hate, and fear); and (c) self-moving; (1) capable of changing environment, (2) capable of manipulating tools, (3) electrochemical (modifies moods through self-induced chemicals), (4) self-expanding structure (cells' differentiation, cultural heredity), (5) delf-moving structure (flexibility as to means, flexibility as to ends), and (6) self-reflexive human is autonomous.

When we come to contextualism, we pass from an analytical into a synthetic type of theory. Characteristic of the synthetic theories that their root metaphors cannot satisfactorily be covered by common sense concepts, common sense is full of animistic, formistic, and mechanistic substances. Contextualism holds tight to the changing and present event. The contextualism categories are derived from what we call the total given event. Disorder is a categorical feature of contextualism (disorder within order). Contextualism is not only about fusion, but about creating new orders of thinking about the human condition. Therefore, the emphasis has to be on the human analogue.

The human analogue, somewhat of a paradox since it applies to itself, in that sense, is not a metaphor. However, we do use it as an analogue to do other things—for example, attributes such as loving, feeling, and rebelling—to nonliving things and animals. The time-binding feature is the most important. We think about thinking, we know that we know. The capacity for introspection, self-examination, self-analysis, and self-criticism puts humans on a higher plane. The human metaphor is constantly in the making. Fixation at any metaphorical level, short of the human analogue, will retard knowledge and dehumanize.

Dr. William J. Williams

Emphasis is on an adequate model of the human being, for the purpose of describing human behavior is not yet out of the developmental and speculative stage. As lower forms are not locked into a particular spatial location, the human is not confined to a particular spatial location. The human is not confined to a particular time frame but will get input from those such as Newton, Aristotle, Ralph Waldo Emerson, Einstein, Planck, Rousseau, Locke, and Russell. Beavers and robins construct their homes from a plan as old as the species. Humans record their experiences in written symbols and are able to improve their recorded experiences. The telephone, video, television, and computer are made to serve as extensions of the human nervous system. An increased self-awareness of self-reflexiveness has to be incorporated into the structure. A human being has the ability to know that he or she knows. Unlike the pigeon, the human can be conditioned and can reflect about being conditioned and escape from the conditioning. Scientific knowledge of the human phenomenon is only as complete as the theoretical constructs and metaphors that describe human behavior.

Contextualism is the key for obtaining nonfragmentation and holism. Once we have moved beyond formism, mechanism, and organicism, our focus is on methods that fit contextualism. Abduction is the key notion and methodological process.

A key notions is abduction, the process introduced by Charles S. Pierce, which embraces deduction and induction. It is a qualitative formulation. It is about postulation; holding findings tentative. It is about creating new symbols, nonmechanical and transactional, instead of interactional, nonfixed ideas and beyond either/or, non-Aristotelian logic, non-Newtonian, nonstatic, nonidentity, and nonallness.

Key terms are transformation, process-like, development, transaction, emergence, complexification, becoming space-time, structural more, field of forces, and self-reflexive. The terms leadership, conflict, motivation, decision making, communication, change, and power are narrow concepts to be engaged and questioned by this mindset for accuracy and adequacy.

The contextual analogy is a very difficult one since there are no road maps. It is a futuristic endeavor. It requires looking at new experiences, not confusing them with old experiences and symbols and then eventually naming them. It also requires looking at old experiences and questioning the appropriateness of symbols and the usefulness of these symbols. The circularity with which we approach this process

New Thinking For A New Millennium

becomes helpful. However, it only helps if we are able to be specific about how to implement key notions as we embrace holism and nonfragmentation—the major forms for future development. We must focus on what is meant by the experience of being feelingly and consciously at one with things, people, and situations. It is not a matter of understanding, of seeing things as the other person does, of adopting an idea because it sounds reasonable, or of joining in an enterprise because it looks practical and practicable. It is a matter of living consciously, at least for a time, in a symbiotic exchange of energy with some dynamic process that affects us at the very depth of our innermost values, attitudes and preferences. Therefore, we have to emphasize the affective rather than the discursive. Then, we are transcursive. It is a full participation that blends thinking, feeling, and all other aspects of our functioning. We should call this participation, which unifies what is fragmental by culture. We have participated in different ways at different stages of human development. Participating has been going on all along. Conscious participating has been the way of dissolving the self-made distance between ourselves and what is going on. Our ancestors did it by using magic, esoteric practices, and religious rituals. We can now, however, learn the art of participating in a consciously guided awareness. A flower blooms or withers according to the time of season. The rooster crows when the dawn begins. The hen cackles when the eggs are laid. The sun appears in the east and disappears in the west. The mountain grows out of the plain. For these to exist is to be at one with activities from which they cannot disassociate. We are not locked up in this manner. I can determine, to some extent, what my participating oneness with the world will be. I can practice this in a variety of ways. I can be at one with this page I am writing, with the painting I spread on canvas, and with a client I help out of a neurosis. We have amplified the sounds of birds into symphonic orchestrations. We have made of simple tribal customs the elaborate systems of our laws and our political institutions. Can we make the art of at oneness a distinct and human creation? Can we devise and practice a oneness that will transform our world of strife and violence into one of harmony? Can we free ourselves of the gravitational pull of separate, individual values and attain mutual trust? Yes, we can, if we learn the secret and practice the skills of being fully at one with physical and biological requirements. How can we do this? We choose a root metaphor that is as similar as possible to the object or situation with which we are dealing. We have, at that time, what is known as a unifying experience.

Dr. William J. Williams

This is easy, of course, to handle with the root metaphors already mapped, but for our contextual metaphor it is more difficult. Then, what do we do? At this stage, we must depend on what the creative scientist depends on; a felt participation with the energy process. We recognize the experience as one that unifies what has been culturally and discursively separated. They come in the form of peak experiences, intentions, bunches, inclinations, feelings, suspicion, and larger "mystical" experiences. This is not new, but if we express these experiences through the formistic, mechanical, or organicism metaphor and syndrome, we will be inappropriate. They take on proper meaning only if we use key notions and terms of the contextual process. To repeat, we must fuse these experiences with the language and ideas of the contextual root metaphor .

When we have a unifying experience where everything comes together, and our *translation* is at a stage below the contextual, that is: postulating, holistic, nonfragmenting, nonelementalistic, non-Aristotelian, we lose the value of the experience. The test is in the translation and interpretation. That is one reason why it is so important to be certain that we maintain a mindset of nonfragmentation and holism. Now, we have come full circle.

The original source for the root metaphors is Pepper's *World Hypotheses*. The original source for the mental models is Boulding's The Image. Many aspects of root metaphors are like the epistemological profile and types of abstracting. Conversely, they are different in many ways. The profile and types of abstracting have an additional stage and are more specific. The mental models are general and more abstract. However, they all can stand alone. One reason I did not combine them into one unit is because I wanted the reader to use them together or separately. To emphasize, while they are similar, there are some major differences. I depart from this point by summarizing as follows: I have outlined five "stages"—one taken from the epistemological profile and the other four from the root metaphors; which, I will call the epistemic unit. This epistemic unit forms the background for what follows.

Part Two:

*Implementation:
The Processes and Application
of Abstracting*

Introduction

The previous chapters were about how to view the old ways of thinking, and how to use methods for creating new symbols and revising old ones that may be inappropriate. It is a matter of mindsets.

We turn now to the identification of a particular method (meticulous) for examining, analyzing and evaluating specific situations. This method, while addressing application, also generates knowledge that can be helpful with our broader objectives of symbol-making and revision of symbols. It is a circular process. Our major objective for this application section is to demonstrate how to apply a method in keeping with the holistic and nonfragmenting thrust that is qualitative, rigorous and meticulous.

That method is labeled the processes of abstracting. The method is broken down into four main divisions: orders of abstraction, types of abstracting, levels of abstracting, and styles of abstracting. The processes of abstracting in the present form are like mathematics and to some extent value-free. However, the translation into substantive application requires that values be added to make the value-free concrete. For example, one drop of water and another drop of water, when kept separate, represents two drops of water. However, when we speak of volume and put the two drops together, the observer sees only one drop. In theory, we have two drops. The same occurs when we talk about the processes of abstracting. Once we identify with processes where something is located, we are value free. Application requires values to change it from a propositional function to a proposition. As a proposition, it is applied and loses the "objectivity."

Chapter Five

Orders of Abstraction—A Diagnosis Propositions and Propositional Functions

Orders are about event, first-order experience, description, interpretation, interpretation of the interpretation, interpretation of the interpretation's interpretation, and so on. This is a discussion of orders of abstraction and how orders work.

In order to analyze and evaluate the various orders, substantively, we apply *levels of abstracting* with *multiordinality* and *types of abstracting*. The application of levels and types makes a rigorous and meticulous analysis of the subject possible. Levels and types will be discussed in chapters six, seven, and eight.

"What is going on," or WIGO, is the basic focus of the processes of abstracting. The WIGO in which we abstract our first-order experience is our own unique world, structured according to our culture and personal experience. According to Bois, being conscious of abstracting, in terms of a first-order experience means: (1) to what we are paying attention, (2) with what we are busy, and (3) with what we are concerned.

When we observe something, we can abstract only a tiny portion of what is going on at any one time. This time observation usually consists of a few seconds. Then, the object or situation we first perceived has changed forever. Things never remain the same. When two different people observe the same things, their observations will usually differ. Our interpretations may vary due to the inherent characteristics we bring into the process. First-order experiences are very personal and dated. Our concern, at a particular point in time, changes very rapidly, as do our impressions of an object or situation.

The maps we construct of our territories, the language we use (whether verbal or nonverbal), and characteristics of time-binding all reveal our own styles of abstracting. Korzybski first presented the map-

New Thinking For A New Millennium

territory distinction in three basic premises of non-Aristotelian logic. The first premise states that the map is not the territory, meaning that words are not the things they represent. The second states that the map does not represent all of the territory; symbols cannot cover everything and, moreover, words cannot say all about anything. Finally, the map is self-reflexive, meaning that a map would have to include a map of a map, and so on. Korzybski states that since the map clearly is not the territory, the only possible relationship between them is structural. The structural association can be further defined by an example: if I took a map into a territory to test its accuracy, I would then be included in that territory, and would subsequently require a new map of myself holding my old map and comparing it with what, to be precise, is not the same territory I had previously mapped.

Korzybski described the process of abstracting as a map and territory. The territory is what is actually going on, while the map is what we abstract from the territory. The map does not represent all the details of the territory. Our maps are comprised of that which we are concerned and interested in at the time. Maps are an abstraction from the territory and a translation of its features into a different medium. We do so from two distinct sources. The first is the present situation that is open to our observations. The second is from the unsorted stock of memories, interpretations, and prejudices that have accumulated within us over the course of our lives. Korzybski also believed that the key to improved, evaluative procedures resides in our "consciousness of abstracting." Korzybski defined "abstracting" as the process proceeding from: (1) event level to object level, (2) object level to the description of it, and (3) one order to a higher order by abstracting characteristics and going from very specific to more general descriptions.

Low-order abstractions are very explicit and descriptive and involve little guessing. The more guessing involved, the further the description is from first-order experience. Low-order abstractions, such as feelings and sensations, are constantly changing, since they are the direct result of contact with the external world which itself is in constant change (Weinberg 1955). Responses to questions that ask who, what, when, or where are low-order abstractions. High-order abstractions describe things with fewer details, using more generalizations. These often tend to oversimplify. Our verbal maps, as opposed to nonverbal maps, become larger, encompassing great territory but providing fewer details as we move up the orders of abstraction. The degree of

Dr. William J. Williams

specificity and detail and the amount of guesswork required are indicators of how high we have traveled up the orders of abstraction.

The major assumption is that this is a natural survival order to the nervous system. If that survival order is violated, we distort our behavior and functioning. In other words, the awareness is about confusing orders of abstraction. The structure of the nervous system consists of ordered chains with the nerve currents that automatically introduce our ordering in a four-dimensional, space-time manifold. A decent respect for the ordered process is necessary if we are to have a structural similarity to the world of events. The emphasis is in our automatic connection between the structure and the event. Transformation requires that the natural order of the nervous system be in sync with the analytical thought process—thus, the value of internalizing this process. Orders of abstraction are about mental and feeling processes. For our purpose here, however, we are confining our discussion to the mechanical application. It would be rude, nevertheless, if I did not make the reader aware that our usage at this juncture "is" just a minor part of orders of abstraction. The circularity and the relations are being left out.

Theoretically, orders of abstraction move us close to the submicroscopic process. Orders, being fundamental, have to do with feelings and the nervous system. In that sense, we are dealing with the event, a first-order experience, and a description of the event. When we invoke orders, we are mainly focusing on two parts, feeling where we are and our interpretations. The moment we insert our interpretations into the equation, we move into more analysis and levels. If, however, the analysis remains mainly analytical and narrow, and for the most part without content, we remain with orders. To illustrate what events, first-order experiences, and descriptions mean in an applied sense, I have chosen to move from a broad abstract discussion about orders and the epistemological underpinnings and focus on the subject of propositions and propositional functions. My charge is to use orders to identify where these fit. Propositional functions can be the first-order experience, and/or second-order and third-order abstractions, and so on. Propositions, however, can only start as a second-order abstraction, simply because the first-order experience is a reaction without symbols. What we want to describe here is that propositions and propositional functions have a structural difference. The process of orders automatically enables us to initially determine the location of the constructs, and later, with the help of levels and types, to determine

New Thinking For A New Millennium

similarities and differences between propositions and propositional functions, one propositional function and another propositional function, and one proposition and another proposition.

The notions of propositions and propositional functions provide us with a way of looking at the mechanical use of orders of abstraction. Russell, in chapter two of *Principia Mathematica,* introduced the theory of types. He posed two orders of abstraction to introduce his method for better understanding the way our thinking is automatically ordered. He observed that we confused first-order with second-order thinking, meaning that we did not separate the orders. He then separated his methods into two parts: propositions and things that function like propositions. He maintained that we often confused propositions with propositional functions, but that if we could understand that they were of different order, our ability to analyze would improve. Certain first-order experiences, descriptions, or statements look like propositions when they are actually propositional functions. A "true" proposition (not a valid one) must be contrary to the Aristotelian system, which makes the following assumptions: (1) that the subject-predicate form of representation can cover scientific and life requirements, (2) there is a belief that all propositions are of the subject-predicate form, and (3) the belief that life and science can be accounted for by propositions that are either true or false.

Grammatically, we may consider a statement a proposition. If couched in the old grammar, it is only a grammatical proposition, not a "true" proposition. Therefore, it should be considered a propositional function if we want more than validity, until it is phrased in the new grammar. Unfortunately, we habitually treat propositional functions as propositions.

Propositional functions are statements that have unspecified, dependent variables, and until they are assigned values they remain propositional functions. Once they receive proper values, we have propositions. Confusing (true) propositions with propositional functions is easy. If propositional functions are stated in the two-valued way, they may be confused with "true" propositions. We have to specify and assign values to make it a "true" proposition. A proposition in grammar may be valid but may not be a proposition in actual life. If it is not, it is ambiguous and thus, in actual fact, is a propositional function. Again, propositions in actual life must have noncompartmentalized and holistic assigned values.

Dr. William J. Williams

Life cannot be accounted for with propositions which are either/or and two valued. Those propositions may be considered valid propositions or propositional functions, because they are only grammatically correct. For a proposition to be considered good, the wording must account for the world of degrees, and be unambiguous and meaningful, or it is only a valid proposition and a propositional function that looks like a "true" proposition. Propositions must be both valid (unambiguous) and "truthful" (actual life-world of degrees).

I will provide an example. There was an intense conflict in a certain Midwestern town over the amount of fluoride in the drinking water. Empirical scientific evidence had been presented to the effect that fluoride in certain proportions reduced tooth decay, but nothing could persuade the town citizens that the fluoride would not be poisonous. The fluoride issue was worded as a propositional function. Fluoride is a deadly poison in sufficient quantities. The measure was worded just in terms of fluoride being put in the water. It was not specific enough. If they had included weights, degrees, and amounts, it would have been a specific statement. Instead, it was a description of fluoride and how it worked. Those that communicated the information talked about it in general. The statement was valid, but not "truthful." It was grammatically correct (Aristotelian- correct and ambiguous).

A "true" proposition, in actual fact, must reflect the values of the independent variable. Simply stated, it must be a contradictory, not a contrary. Propositional functions or valid propositions are contraries that frequently look like contradictories.

Identifying and analyzing the dependent variable is the first step in keeping these distinctions clear and opening the way for better diagnosing. More precise diagnosing is assured by levels and types of abstracting (the independent variables).

In Summary

Below are three elements we should engage in our business with orders of abstraction:

1. Determine mechanically whether or not the issue, program, person, or policy is first-order experience, description, or interpretation. We can determine this by applying these words: the first-order experience is the first impact from the event (not words); the second order is what we say about the first order; and the third order is what we can say about the second (interpretation).

New Thinking For A New Millennium

2. The second order can become a propositional function or a proposition; that is, a description or an interpretation of the first-order experience. The determining factor is *how* it is said.
3. The recognition begins with an evaluation of the structure of each order. We should observe the following principles: propositional functions propositions—(a) the law of identity, antidote: law nonidentity; (b) the law of noncontradiction, antidote: self-reflexiveness; (c) the law of the excluded middle, antidote: nonallness; (d) the law of permanency, antidote: the principle of process; and (e) contraries, antidote: contradictories.

Following these principles will guarantee a rigorous, qualitative assessment as a prelude to a more in-depth analysis and evaluation. Clearly, if we apply the language of orders of abstraction, we mechanically do not confuse orders of abstractions, thereby eliminating early conflicts and unsolvable verbal difficulties.

Orders are designed to reorder the nervous system, or in other words, to restore it to a natural order—for example, when we confuse these orders, such as propositions with propositional functions and first-order experience with second-order descriptions. The orders will bring this to our attention, and diagnosing becomes automatic and more accurate.

Finally, a good example of confusing orders of abstraction is when we get into affirmative action. A person recommends that we do a set-aside for women and/or minorities. The response is to negatively label the set-aside as a quota. The introducing of the quota argument is a third-order abstraction, and the idea about a set-aside is a second-order abstraction, the descriptive order. There is no need to move to the third order. By doing this, we confuse orders of abstraction and end up discussing the label rather than the subject.

We can readily see just by using orders that the second and third orders are different and, by definition, should not be confused. However, that diagnosis alone does not help us to qualitatively analyze either order as to whether we are dealing with propositions or propositional functions. The determination is made by introducing levels and types of abstracting. Thus, we are led to a redefining of the usage of the processes of abstracting based on a calculus epistemological underpinning. The equation $y = f(x)$ designates propositional functions and propositions. For our purpose here, y in the equation remains a propositional function until values are assigned through x, which will represent levels and types of abstracting. Orders are like premises taken from syllogistic reasoning. The deductive processes need to be analyzed to determine whether they are propositions or propositional functions. Once the determination is made, implementation is the next phase. There are two aspects to implementation: what we derive from our analysis and how we use it. To repeat, this requires a mechanical application of the independent variables (*levels* and *types*) to dependent variables (*orders*).

Illustration 1

Abstraction Diagram
Orders of Abstraction

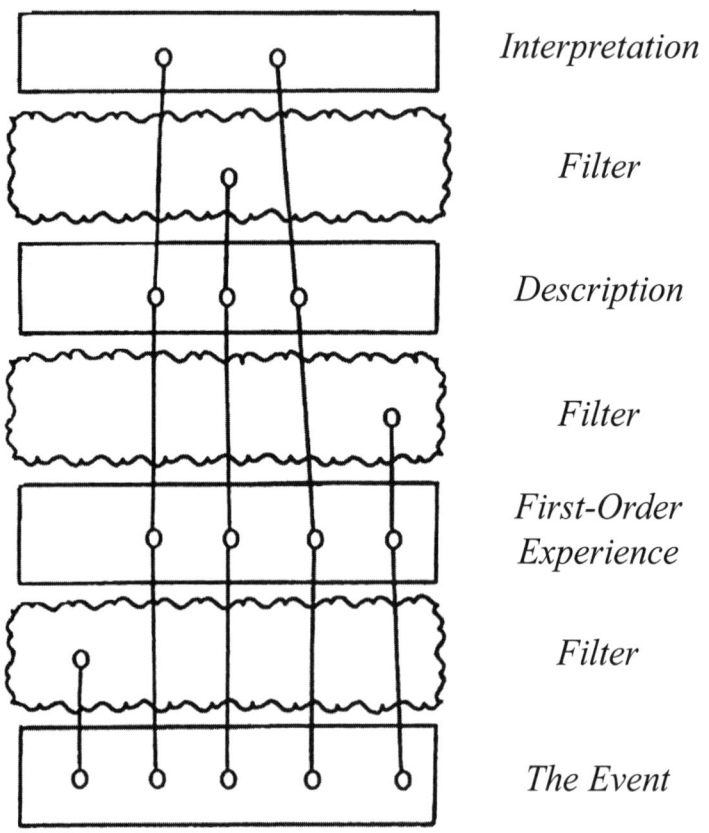

Chapter Six
Types of Abstracting: Diagnosis, Evaluation and Analysis

Types of abstracting is our second focus. As we move from one type to the next, the subjects' definition as well as meaning changes. Types differ from orders. Types carry some substance, and our analysis with orders is strictly mechanical. Orders tell us where. The insertion of types enables us to insert the what; that is, meaning of the order. With orders, we merely report one "order" from another without making judgments, other than the judgment about not confusing one order with another. Types are about evaluation.

Types of abstracting transcend logic and represents broader subjects. The meaning and definition of each succeeding type of abstracting emphasizes a difference in "kind." The four different types of abstracting are separate and distinct in their workings. The first type is sensing and is characterized by reactions. Classifying is the second type of abstracting, in which structure and actions take place. The third type is relating and is identified through interactions. Finally, postulating is the fourth type where transactions and transformations take place. To repeat, the meaning and dictionary definition of each word or statement changes with each of the four different types. In contrast, with levels only, the meaning changes but the definition remains the same.

The first type of development is the sensing type. Here, our reactions are evaluative (parallel to the levels of abstracting). The world is sensed as beautiful or depressing and controlled by the moods of the gods. Type one is characterized by "chitchat," or an explosive statement. There is no intention to communicate. Thinking is one-dimensional. In sum, no one really benefits too much on both the giving and, especially, the receiving ends. It is reactive and pre-Aristotelian. I react because all blacks are lazy or all whites are racist. It may be all in

New Thinking For A New Millennium

my head. There is a belief in logic and reaction to words; that is, communism or capitalism. We react to messages and our reactions are signal, not symbolic.

In type-two classifying, we see the world not controlled by the whims of the gods but by its own nature and being and its own equilibrium. This state is indicative of logical classification. The qualities of the world may change, but the substance, the world itself, does not. There is permanence. The world has an essence. In language, this state is reflected by humans as the "things they say *are* really *are*." "Things are what our language says they are." Type two is under the impression that the collective brain of this culture mirrors the world; for each word in the dictionary there is a corresponding fact, a person, or an action. If their thinking goes from one thought to another according to the rules of logic, they are sure that it goes from one fact to another in the real world. Within their brain there is a miniature world. Whenever we take as ultimate truth a "clear," "positive" notion, we think at type two. Whenever we think in terms of opposites, we are of the classifying type. The difference between type one and type two is not a matter of instruments but is a matter of what we call "objectivity." For humans functioning at type two, things are what our language says they are. This is about deduction. We deduce about homosexuality, and from certain premises we generalize about it. Our approach to understanding is logical. It is about logic. The definitions change from type one to thinking in terms of subject-predicate in type two. In type one, there was no thinking, just acceptance. In levels there is an acceptance of the definition of homosexuality on all levels. In type two we do not accept the reactive premise of homosexuality. We draw conclusions from a different premise. Thus, there is a difference between type two and level two. In type two the "message itself" is focused upon. Attention is given to the "sending card" of the communication, with little emphasis on the receiving process. The verb "to be" is of major importance. An attempt is made to use words to make the map come to life as the actual territory. We make use of the etiquette of public speaking—of styles and gestures. This is the world Aristotle codified. It is about categories and classifying. There is a single cause for an effect. Some terms to apply are status, essence, structural hierarchy, balance, monument, substance, observer, space, subject-predicate, permanence, definition, problems, fact, consistency, and addition.

In type three, the relating type, the dictionary definition and the meaning of what we do, think, and evaluate changes. We do not talk

Dr. William J. Williams

about homosexuality, but humansexuality. This is about sexuality in general and relationships. Homosexuality becomes a particular case and is now part of the world of interaction as various elements interact with each other mechanically. In type three, the receiving end is focused upon. The mentality, education, and attitudes of the listener are taken into account. It is the world of facts and values with a connection. The world of logical positivism is dominant. The use of microscopes and machines of energy are indicative of type three. The world is seen as a complex of interrelated parts—as a huge machine whose workings we keep discovering one after the other—and we learn to control the . . . more efficiently. We long ago gave up the naive notion that there is a single cause for any single phenomenon. We know that whatever happens is due to the convergence of many antecedents. For many persons this is the top achievement, and science becomes the supreme value. To oppose science is to be a heretic in today's world. This is the world of Descartes, Newton, and Bacon. Some terms to apply are dynamic, function, interaction, causality, machine, energy, self-improvement, space and time, entropy, smooth-running, manipulation, asymmetry, function, multiplication, and doing.

Type four consists of much more abstract formulations. Here, we understand that the world we strive to control in type three is not the whole picture. We become aware of our limitations. With the postulating type, we are conscious that whatever laws of nature we know are tentative. In type-four communication, feedback is transcended. The sender goes beyond the requirements of the audience into a "vital transaction," where both parties feel involved with the sender, the message itself, and the audience. Thoughts, attitudes, and interests are in "sensitive contact." It is a self-reflexive state of communication into which the communicator is aware of the limits of his or her observations and, therefore, invites participation in discussion which is open-ended so that a better map may be attempted. The key terms in type four are transaction, transformation and abduction assisted by specific nonelementalistic, nonfragmenting, and holistic functions designed to enable us to meticulously and rigorously apply the key terms. The terms to apply are transformation, process-like, emergence, field of forces, time, space-time, structural more, participants, self-renewal, and transaction. In addition to change in definition and meaning with each type, types offer a challenge to the existing name of the subject and suggests symbol change. We inaugurate an epistemological investigation substantively and symbolically. This makes it uniquely type four. This is the world of changing and engaging what we call something. The symbols are engaged and the names change. This is the world of Einstein, Planck, relativity, quantum, and beyond physics. The example of homosexuality as it pertains to type four is discussed below.

Differences in kind is the hallmark of *types of abstracting*. The differences in kind means each type is autonomous and each *type* makes a particular case of the previous stage. We note that the dictionary *definitions* and *meanings* change as we go from one stage of typing to another. The key terms here are *stages* and *typing*. Concerning levels, the key term is *level*.

How would this play out in our rigorous analysis with levels, which moves us from analysis to evaluation? Analysis becomes a particular case within evaluation, except when we use one level to analyze the overall nature of types. Levels can be considered the container at that point, rather than the content. This rigorous analysis process is circular. It defies the law of noncontradiction and, therefore, can be both *a* and *b*.

To continue our evaluation, let us now evaluate homosexuality. In type one we just react to homosexuality. This is the reaction stage. In type two we discuss sexual preferences; definitions are static, inflexible, and fixed. You either are homosexual or you are not. Nevertheless, it is about sexual preference. The theme at this stage is about logic, meaning there is only one kind. The ideas are nonfunctional, Aristotelian, fixed, static, and either/or. The dictionary definition and meanings change from type one. We are discussing, at this point, sexual preferences—a stage of objectivity.

In type three we talk about sexuality, making homosexuality a particular case again. The dictionary definition and the meaning simultaneously change. This is the relating type. It is mechanical, embracing countless connections and many kinds of homosexuality.

We move next to the postulating type. (We talk about name change.) Remember, earlier I wrote that our analysis with levels within each type could only go so far. To take our homosexual analysis beyond the third type requires analyzing and evaluating with a process beyond the criteria of *levels of abstracting*. The summary questions posed at this point is: what evaluations are rendered by using *types of abstracting* and *levels of abstracting* as analysis and, how dow we analyze the postulating type without having *levels* as a tool for analysis?

All statements from our level of rigorous analysis are within types one, two, and three. Most of the thinking, in other words, regarding

Dr. William J. Williams

homosexuals, falls within types one, two, and three: reactive (sensing), static-fixed (active), and mechanical (interactive). With type four (postulating) we question the use of the term homosexuality and hold the term tentative. Moreover, we move positively in the direction of implementing new ways of symbolizing and talking about homosexuality. We question the use of the term and the category. We lean toward human transactions. The key term here is transaction.

Thus far, we have talked about diagnoses (orders) and evaluation (types). They are not mutually exclusive. They must be taken together. When we begin with types, we are automatically diagnosing and analyzing. In order to make it rigorous and meticulous, we have to insert levels specifically into the equation. Conversely, some evaluation and analysis takes place with the use of orders but, alone, it does not give the meticulousness and overall evaluation. The same is evident with types. Some evaluation and diagnosis takes place, but the analysis is not dimensional and the diagnosing is not explicit. These processes must be used in conjunction with each other.

All of this should lead to application, examining of a subject, understanding of a subject, developing of ideas about a subject, and to measuring, by a set of criteria, the significance and importance of what is examined and measured. Now, we will move to the application of levels.

Chapter Seven

*Levels of Abstracting:
Analysis*

Levels of abstracting in the context in which I am writing serve as one of the tools for analyzing and evaluating orders of abstraction and the content of types of abstracting. It is, in a certain respect, a conversion process. The values assigned to levels are applied to orders and enable us to do a more meticulous analysis with types. Simultaneously, levels serve as a diagnostic process, since they are also a part of the interpretive circular process. Some of the same key terms used to describe levels are applied to types, with one distinction in mind: levels address differences in degree and types address differences in kind. The use of *multiordinality* is confined to levels, since multiordinality deals with degrees. *Multiordinality* is simply a way of saying we move terms, subjects, and ideas from one level to another, without changing definition, but the meanings change.

We can use the map-territory analogy to describe the role of levels. Orders become the broad outline of the territory (the forest). Types insert the next step (the trees), and levels provide the next step (branches and leaves). I might add here that the accuracy and adequacy of the values of the levels will determine how well the objectives are carried out. In other words, oversimplified, orders are about where, types are about what, and levels are about how. There must be a consistency between the broad perspective, philosophy, policy, and/or intended goal. Let me use another analogy to explain. Suppose a patient needed a heart transplant. This would be the order, the intended goal and the territory. Our map would be types and levels. The kind of heart chosen is important. It must be compatible with the territory (the person). The kind of heart must be typed properly and the ingredients that go into typing would be levels. All matches must be in order if the heart is to work, or it will be rejected. The same applies with other matters. If the values assigned are not in conformity with the territory, the maps being designed under the auspices of types and levels will not make for a successful implementation. Therefore, in order to accomplish the task of analysis, we need to: (1) define the characteristics peculiar to each level and (2) utilize a tool called multiordinality to aid us with our analysis. We use both in the following manner: we apply the total notion of levels (the defined characteristics) to each order of abstraction we are analyzing. In other words, it is a way, mechanically and substantively, to not confuse one level with another. The y (orders) become propositions when we do the following: $y = f(l + t)$.

To use levels, the notion of *multiordinality* is necessary. Defined, it simply means we move the subject, whatever it is, from one level to another with meaning changes, while the definition of the subject remains the same. To repeat, *multiordinality* is a guide to noting meaning changes as we do the analysis.

The multiordinality of terms refers to the ability to use the *same dictionary definition* but reflects different *meanings* at different levels of abstracting. This places levels and *multiordinality* within the vertical aspects of our thinking. They can easily move from a lower order to a higher order, from specific to general. This ability also allows *multiordinal* terms to serve as the content, or the container. Most subjects, such as policies, programs, issues, racism, feminism, codependency, homosexuality, heterosexuality, Democratic Party, Republican Party, and Independent Party, have different meanings as each is taken through different levels of abstracting. To confuse one level with another would be mixing levels, as well as orders, and our analysis would be qualitatively weak. Quantitative analysis will not usually allow for comparison of different levels. It will usually have one definition and meaning made explicit. This is precisely the weakness of quantitative analysis. By inserting the multiordinal instrument into the equation, we embark upon rigorous qualitative analysis. I will describe the various levels now and return later to a more precise analysis of the notion of homosexuality, by which the same method can be used to analyze other notions like racism, policy, codependency, and so on. You will see that the similar syndromes and terms are used for types and levels. The difference is in the levels the subject under discussion maintains the same *dictionary definition*, emphasizing *meaning* changes (degrees) and with types the subject under discussion requires *definition* and *meaning* changes This is the *major difference* between *levels* and *types*.

Dr. William J. Williams

Evaluative level abstracting is a matter of sensing and feeling. We take the feel of our reactions as the adequate map of objective reality. Things are either good or bad. The major notion used here is reaction. There is a lack of structure. There is no categorizing in intellectual terms. We deal with notions like freedom, liberty, democracy, beauty, religion, spirituality, God, happiness, good, bad, criminal, and so on. This is an intentionally oriented level, unspecific, using high order abstractions (statements) as low-order abstractions.

At the classifying level, we have a world of words. Classifying abstracting allows us to categorize "facts" or objects in "kind" according to their similarities or commonalities with one another. This can be found in static symbols. The terms elements and framework are key. It is not just classifying, but it is also imbued with the law of identity. A thing is either *a* or *b,* and cannot be both *a* and *b.* The abstracting is dead-level, with no content and one container. It is either/or. It is about sameness. It is about elementalism at this level. This is Aristotelian and fixed logic, static thinking, and deductive reasoning.

There are two components within the classifying level of abstracting. One is about concrete matters that do not have broader implications. There is the one man. We do not see differences nor similarities with other categories. We cannot, with this primitive and animalistic categorizing, create larger categories or more refined categories. However, with objective classifying we see *sameness*. We can rise from one level or category to another. *Differences* are left out. At the primitive level, there is one kind of classifying. One kind of racism is the same as another kind. One kind of codependency is the same as any other kind. One kind of homosexuality is the same as another kind.

Objective abstracting allows us to put our classification of the second level above into "family containers." The simple classifications are the content of the container. The key terms for this classifying are structure, form, static, essence, hierarchy, balance, substance, monument, consistency, observer, object, and subject-predicate. There is a term we should submit as an identifying point, and that term is *action*.

Relating abstracting is the third level. We function according to what is now called the scientific method. We discover how the elements of a situation are actually related to one another, and we express those relations in a mathematical formulas. There is a key term that we should insert as an identifying point, and that term is interaction. Some other terms to look for at this level in our analysis are action, space and time, doing, self, self-improvement, smooth-running, and feedback. This is the mechanical. The notion of feedback is prominent, as reflected in the age of Nicolaus Copernicus, Galileo, William Harvey, Johannes Kepler, Baruch Spinoza, Descartes, Newton, and Bacon.

The next level of abstracting is unifying abstracting. At this point, "We are aware of our awareness," not simply that we do exist, but that we are aware that we exist. The key term for this is integration. Other terms are affiliations, merging, fact-value, structure-functions, psychosomatic, body-mind, black-white, thinking-feelings, public-private, and so on. This process is called nonelementalistic, as reflected in the Age of Logical Positivism (Ludwig Wittgenstein). This part of our rigorous, meticulous analysis aids us in identifying the quality of the order of abstraction and the typing. We begin, as we do our meticulous analysis, to encounter processes that do not fit our definitions for types. For example, the levels along with the accompanying instrument of multiordinality are designed to reveal information about those processes that are bounded by a fixed dictionary definition with meaning changes at different levels, and to examine those processes (within orders and types) that do and do not change meanings and definitions simultaneously. Levels lead to a more rigorous analysis, because we then talk about a confrontation with our categories and labels, and the history and emergence of the categories and terms. I am writing about them separately, but they are used in conjunction with others as we do our rigorous, meticulous analysis.

Now, I will return to an analysis of homosexuality as an example of how the imposition of levels work. Homosexuality is a statement beyond the description. In other words, it is three orders removed from the event itself. There is the first-order experience, then the description. The label homosexual is not even a description, so in analysis I learned by looking at orders that it is just a label, or a classification. It is of the classifying type. It is static. It is subject-predicate. Whatever is said about homosexuality at that order and within that type is just a map that has very little to do with the territory, which is the event. It flows from a first-order experience but skips description. It is the *is of identity*. It is *elementalistic*. At this level homosexuality is static. It is fixed. It says all homosexuality is the same. It is Aristotelian. It is a subject-linking–verb-noun. It observes the law of noncontradiction. It is a propositional function, and yet a grammatical "proposition."

Dr. William J. Williams

When we move to objective classifying, we see homosexuality as belonging to a larger group of activities, called "gay." It is also a strict classification leaving out many details. We then move to the relating level to examine the term, and we find here that the interpretation is not stilted. The notion of homosexuality is related to other humans. The notion is no longer static. The relating level is a study of relationships. Different questions are being posed. Homosexuality becomes dynamic, and one cannot be put in a neat category. It transcends either/or, which says you are homosexual or you are not. A homosexual can be a Republican, Democrat, layman, doctor, or clerk. Other relationships are considered. It is the level of interaction. A homosexual is just a part of a larger process. It is more of the descriptive order but still a propositional function, as far as "truth," but from the standpoint of validity, a proposition. This level is beyond the classifying level where gay means gay (dead-level abstracting). Then, we move to the unifying level where homosexuality is a talk about humans. The meaning changes. It is about merging changes. It is about merging men-women. It is about man having feminine as well as masculine tendencies. It is about females having both male and female hormones. We no longer see this as being either/or. Homosexuality is different but not negatively so. The word homosexual does not say all about the person. It is only a label. This becomes a proposition, but not a "true" proposition, since the definition is not engaged. It is still just valid and remains a grammatical proposition only. It is a statement more like a descriptive order of abstracting. What has our analysis brought about up to this point? Mainly, it concludes that the label itself is an oversimplification and has no real meaning. It is subject-predicate. It is either/or, fixed, narrow, and static. Since the definition does not change, all levels discussed fit within the classifying and relating types.

Types have already been discussed in the previous chapter. Qualitatively, levels enable us to determine what homosexuality would mean at different levels of abstracting, within the typing. Quantitative analysis would automatically leave homosexuality as a part of the classifying type. Levels as qualitative rigorous analysis expands the analysis. The meanings would change, but the definition remains the same. Levels analysis is a method for understanding a more rigorous use of flexibility. We make explicit our method and, in practical terms, show how quantitative analysis locks our mind, as well as how we can communicate processes that will help the average person develop political, economic, and social ideas that may enable us to function, in

New Thinking For A New Millennium

general, more sanely. In short, it shows us where the notions reside as stated and how we may be able to view them in a different manner. As stated, the notion of homosexuality provides one definition and meaning and was designed as such. Levels show the limitation of that definition. In other words, the qualitatively used levels is a way of explaining the understanding of an original statement.

At the evaluative, classifying level of abstracting, (black-white, either/or), you are either homosexual or you are not. At the objective step of classifying abstracting, it is still either black or white or good and bad homosexuals. Nonetheless, it is more inclusive classifying. At the relating level good and bad come together. There is a recognition of both aspects. They interact with each other, whereby one aspect acts upon another. The definition remains the same. Only meanings change. The stereotype is fixed even though we have moved to a different level.

At the unifying level of abstracting, we see homosexuality as having some kind of relationship with heterosexuality, lesbians, bisexuals, transvestites, and so on. The key term here is integration. Relationships can be formed in many different ways. Homosexuals are no different than heterosexuals; good and bad and either/or lose their meanings. However, the dictionary definition remains. There is still something called homosexuality. By using this analysis, I can determine what someone is thinking on this issue and, many times, it may reflect itself in the developing of not only personal thinking but public policy.

The commonality between all of these levels is that the *definition* does not change. We are still talking about homosexuality. However, the *meaning* of homosexuality *does* change.

1. Evaluative: reaction
2. Classifying: action
3. Relating: interaction
4. Unifying: integration

The viewing of the subject is different at each level, less restrictive and more flexible. Up to this point, we can safely conclude that our qualitative analysis renders the term homosexuality as jargon and pseudo-knowledge. Moreover, it is a propositional function rather than a proposition. We could do the same for racism, codependency, or any issue. The qualitative process of levels would, by utilizing the syndromes of the levels, dictate the statements we make at each of our levels of analysis. What we are finding as we use our levels is that

Dr. William J. Williams

conceptual notions like dysfunction, addiction, and codependency, once relatively clear diagnostic categories, apply to almost anything one does too much of too often. Such indiscriminate use of terminology creates jargon. These hardened metaphors all substitute for good thinking and are premature certitude substitutes for an analysis with practical value.

We must remember, as we close our specific discussion about levels, that levels, unlike types of abstracting, are not about "truth," "honesty," "adequacy," and "accuracy," but about "precision," "validity," "logic," and differences and similarities as matters of degree. It is a meticulous analysis of the type decisions. Levels give the gradations and components of the broad typing. The weaknesses and strengths of the typing are revealed, thereby, to some extent, determining feasibility of application and the relationship of the elements to the overall goal of "typing."

Chapter Eight

Fusion:
Integration and Rigorous Analysis

Mary Parker Follette wrote in the fields of social science, creativity, management theory and behavior. She wrote on a variety of subjects, including leadership, conflict and decision-making. I will quote her verbatim and do the analysis through orders, types and levels.

Before I launch into Follette, I will acquaint you with a background frame for the criteria we use to guide our analyses. Annexed to what we already use are:

1. What kind of structure is being used? For example, how is the material arranged? Was it mechanical? In other words, what was the container; that is, syllogistic, mechanical, scientific or postulative.
2. What is the substance? Is the content mechanical, scientific, Aristotelian, or postulative.
3. What is the method of inquiry behind the statement? For example, is the epistemological underpinning Aristotelian, Newtonian, Einsteinian or postulative.

These breakdowns identify and structure a focus for our analysis. I will use my processes to diagnose, analyze, and evaluate Follette's way of dealing with conflict. The first example is about conflict.

Example Number One

"There are three main ways of dealing with conflict: domination, compromise and integration. Domination is a victory of one side over the other. The second way is compromise. It is the way we settle most of our controversies. Each side gives up a little in order to have peace or . . . in order that the activity which has been interrupted by the conflict may go on. The third is integration . . . that means that two desires are integrated and a solution is found in which both desires have found a place, that neither side has had to sacrifice anything" (Fox and Urwick 1977).

(Comment: This is not a story about the feasibility of the usage of the above processes. Our job is to demonstrate the usage of the qualitative analysis system we are introducing. In other words, can we use our system to determine the value of the statement made by the author?)

Analysis Number One

The application of orders tells us that these are descriptive statements. It is not the event. It is not a first-order experience. It is a description. This is what orders tell us. Now, we superimpose types of abstracting. We know that domination conflict is of the sensing type, because it is about something or someone being acted upon. There are no choices. If you reread the syndrome for the sensing type, it will bear this out. It is not a matter of choosing. You are either dominated or dominating. You do not have a choice. It is a reactive process, one way. Subordinates are always subordinate and dominated, and superiors are superior. It is dead-level abstracting.

The second advocates compromise in conflict. It is either/or and therefore, the classifying type. In this type there are no shades of gray. It is a matter of choosing one or the other. It is fixed—either black or white, static and inflexible, logical and Aristotelian.

The third is integration, which is of the relating type. It is a state of interaction in which things act upon each other. Parts fit together. The machine model is mechanical, but it does provide alternatives, and the parts are all related. There is, however, something about integration that speaks to synthesis, or pulling things together in a unified whole. To classify this (integration) as totally within the relating type becomes difficult, because integration is about unity. When things are unified and synthesized, they may change form or be transformed. In order to make our analysis more accurate in a case where a particular notion or issue, for example, may not fit perfectly within a type, we must employ another instrument. Thus, we turn to levels.

Levels have four steps. Level one, evaluating; level two, classifying; level three, relating; and level four, unifying (holding the key to a more refined analysis).

When we look at domination with levels, we find that the concept has a limited meaning. It does not move beyond the evaluating and classifying levels and, therefore, fits snugly within the sensing type. The notion of compromise fits within the classifying and relating levels. Since there is something about compromising that offers alternatives, it may not be one or the other. Compromise could consist of choosing from more than two choices. That would qualify it for a higher level, but not a higher type. It would still be the relating type. This is a way of satisfying any confusion when it appears that a conceptual notion, process, or issue may not appear to fit snugly within the type predominantly identified. The inclusion of level enables us to accommodate the so-called "overflow" when we put something within types. However, it is not mutually exclusive, and some minor part may appear to place a process within another type. Since we are concerned not only about preponderance but also about precision, levels enable us to put the conceptual notion into proper perspective. Consequently, compromise may be at the classifying and relating levels, but only of the classifying type. Likewise, while integration fits within the relating type, which resembles postulating, we can quickly resolve the dilemma by introducing the levels, which puts integration at the unifying level. Instead of having the notion hang between relating and postulating types, we institute levels and find that we can comfortably include it within the relating type, putting integration there and dealing with integration at the unifying level, since it does not fit comfortably within the postulating type.

The postulating type calls for some things that are not inherent in integration of conflict. They are:

1. Flexibility in terminology, whereby the phrase integration of conflict is fixed and, therefore, not flexible
2. Holding tentative the notion of conflict itself, and necessitating a substitution representing not only a meaning change, but a change in definition
3. Satisfying the requirement of transformation

As you may have noticed above, when talking about the notion of conflict and Follette's statement, she never mentioned the elimination of the word conflict. If a process is to qualify for the postulating type, it must talk about a change in terms; that is, Follette continued to talk about conflict. In types, the definition must change. Conflict must lose its dictionary definition if integrating conflict is to qualify for the postulating type. As it stands, to repeat, it can only qualify for the

New Thinking For A New Millennium

unifying level. Levels do, however, give more precision and qualitative rigor.

Example Number Two

"If anyone thinks that the distinction between power over and power with is a fanciful or personal distinction, I am pleased to be able to say that these two propositions are used to mark a distinction in law. . . . I have sometimes wondered whether it would be better to give up the word 'leader' since to so many it suggests merely the leader-follower relation. But it is far too good a word to abandon. . . . The invidiousness of power over is very well illustrated by Gandhi. Surely his method of noncooperation was a use of power. The nonpayment of taxes . . . Gandhi made declaration of war to the end. Well war is war . . . calls his struggle a war of the spirit . . . I think we should try to abolish the war image" (Fox and Urwick 1977).

Analysis Number Two

(a) The processes: in the first instance above, power over versus power with, the abstract order would be descriptive. However, the evaluation of the quality of the description is dependent upon types and levels. No matter how laudable the idea, the structure is still of the classifying type. It pits one against the other— power over versus power with. However, to do a more meticulous analysis, I insert levels. Levels enable us to evaluate the substance within the classifying type. I find that power over is of the classifying type and level. Power with is of the relating type and on the unifying level. It is action (classifying type— power over) and interaction (relating type—power with) and unifying level.

(b) The next example is about the term leadership. First, Follette said, "I have sometimes wondered if it would be better to give up the word 'leader' . . . [then she added] but it is far too good a word to abandon." She came to the "water" and refused to "swim" when she added the latter statement. The suggestion that we should give up the word leader, if left alone, would have put us in the postulating type. This type has as one of its components the engaging of symbols—definition, meanings, and what we call something has to be changed in order to represent the differences in kind and the new development. A good example is when Einstein called his new development "relativity" rather than "Newtonian plus," and he did not call quantum "relativity plus." It is a move from interaction to transaction. It is a transformation

Dr. William J. Williams

or a structural more, not just an addition. Unfortunately, Follette failed to meet all of the criteria for the postulating type, because when the latter statement, "It is far too good a word to abandon," is added, she is deprived of residence within the postulating type. Thus, she is marooned within the relating type. The refusal to engage the term for elimination becomes an anchoring to the past. The meticulous analysis with levels, however, moves the statement to the unifying level. Levels are about differences in degree, and this degree is created by a lack of the elimination of the word leadership. An abandonment of it would have been a difference in kind, and not of degree, thereby moving it to type four.

(c) The statement, however, about Gandhi is complete. It satisfied the requirement of the postulating type, which demands that we be creative, innovative, and new in kind, not just in degree. Follette, in this instance, says "war is war." We should try to abolish the war image. This is completed and finds its way to the postulating type. Its residence is secured within type four. However, the introduction of levels shows that the statement is dead-level abstracting, meaning one kind of war is not the same as another, but does not minimize the intent of the statement. We do not need to introduce levels in order to find a place for the statement. Its residence is secured.

By using these modes of analysis, we do several things:

1. We are able to distinguish propositional functions from propositions by assigning values and weights to qualitative processes; something, heretofore, left to quantitative analysis
2. We internalize a system that enables us to do analysis automatically
3. We retrain our nervous systems and prepare for situations that are simple and complex
4. We enable ourselves to make explicit our assumptions and the methods we are using
5. We will be able to understand ourselves and the world around us
6. We will be able to share with less difficulty our ideas, feelings, thoughts, and motives
7. We will be able to communicate more effectively

New Thinking For A New Millennium

8. We will be able to interpret and divulge the bases for our interpretations

9. We will be able to skillfully make judgments about opinions and know when one opinion is better than another

10. We will be able to share a system with others

11. Finally, we will know where we are coming from, know where others are coming from, create new ways of functioning, and become effective decision makers while we are wed to the process of change

The processes are not mutually exclusive. They are intricately fused. However, in order to illustrate the workings of the total process and make it understandable, let me repeat my objective, which is to do qualitative, rigorous, meticulous analysis pursued through orders, levels, and types of abstracting.

Let's look at how we began. We outlined orders, levels, and types, and used the subject of homosexuality as a focal point. We could have used any subject, such as affirmative action, sexism, racism, codependency, heterosexuality, national health insurance, abortion, and/or any social, psychological, political, or economic issue. Let's not focus on the example chosen. It is the process we are attempting to communicate. I chose homosexuality because it is a subject I had never put through the process. I wanted to test the theory that we could randomly select a subject we know nothing about and test the qualitative, rigorous, meticulous analysis of our inquiry methods.

In terms of orders, the subject of homosexuality was not mentioned because orders are about diagnosing and, by definition, general and noncontent, but now we will address it. In the first instance, we would differentiate the event, the first-order experience, and the description. The first-order experience would determine the kind of description. The subject is mentioned, and we automatically set in motion types and levels. What we want to determine is what kind of behavior or words are expressed pertaining to the subject. We immediately and automatically dissect that first-order experience through the description. We involve types of abstracting. If we find that it is of the first-type variety, which is sensing, we insert into the process the notion of levels to determine the level of thinking within that type.

Let's look at the statements, "Homosexuals are not born. They are made. Homosexuals react to each other and the behavior is reinforced

Dr. William J. Williams

through interaction." The analysis: the language should be observed first. The use of the term react is of the sensing type; and, in the second part of the statement, the term interaction is used. This is the relating type. The language suggests that the thinking is pre-Aristotelian (primitive), and the machine model (interactive) emerging out of seventeenth-century processes (Bacon and Newton). The structure is grammatically and logically a proposition, but in "truth," it is a propositional function. Structure puts it in the classifying type, which arises out of Aristotelian thinking well within the 650–350 B.C. mindset. The structure is linear cause to effect. It says that homosexuals are made through a reactive and interactive process. The substance of the statement which asserts that homosexuals are not born but are made, is an absolute statement with no flexibility. It comes from a mindset that is fixed and buried in a philosophy that does not entertain shades of gray. Whatever I say it is, it is. This is the is of identity, the epistemological underpinning emerging out of classificatory Aristotelian thinking and promoted in our grammar. Our evaluation which determined that this overall statement was the classifying type does not change unless, at some point, the beginning definition of homosexuality changes. Although we might find elements that would appear to suggest a different type of thinking, we must be concerned with what is predominant. We would move the type to the second type of classifying because of the description and the statement beyond the description. In total, the epistemological inquiry methods used to produce this statement are pre-rationality (650–350 B.C.) thinking, subject-predicate (Aristotelian), and the seventeenth-century machine model. If we were to include the root metaphor of Pepper, the mindsets would be formistic and mechanical. Further testament to the universality of the inquiry methods we are using to analyze and identify inquiry methods of the statement above, are the works of Boulding and Bridgeman. Boulding supplied us with the mental models. The mental models (framework and clockwork) are similar to the levels and stages of abstracting we used above. In the case of Bridgeman, the first and second conceptual revolutions are representing the ideas of Aristotle (the first) and Bacon and Newton (the second conceptual revolution). These two inquiry methods, to some extent, provide us with justification.

At this point I will introduce the format for implementation of analysis and evaluation of whatever policy, program, individual, or action process we should encounter. We should be guided as follows:

New Thinking For A New Millennium

1. Determine what the author of the statement(s) is saying and the way it is being said
2. Analyze the stated objectives and the structure of the statement(s) to determine where the various symbols fit and what the author says the stated symbols mean
3. Look for the inquiry methods that are made explicit (secondary) and offered by the author, if any
4. Look for the inquiry methods that are implicit and epistemological and those that are not made explicit
5. Look for the connection between what the author says he or she wants to do and how it is to be accomplished. In other words, do the inquiry methods, explicit and implicit, enable the author to achieve the stated objectives? More specifically, do the methods match the stated goals? For example, are the goals in type four and the methods in type four, or are the methods in type three and the goals in type four, and so on?

Illustration 2*

An Integrated Comparison

Examination	Meticulous Analysis	Evaluating with Rigor
<u>Orders</u> **	<u>Levels</u>	<u>Types</u>
Statement, Statement		
Description, First-order Experience		
WIGO *** (Event)	Unifying	Postulating
	Relating	Relating
	Classifying	Classifying
	Evaluative	Sensing

* *Please read from bottom to top*
** *An order may be of any level and/or type*
*** *What is going on*

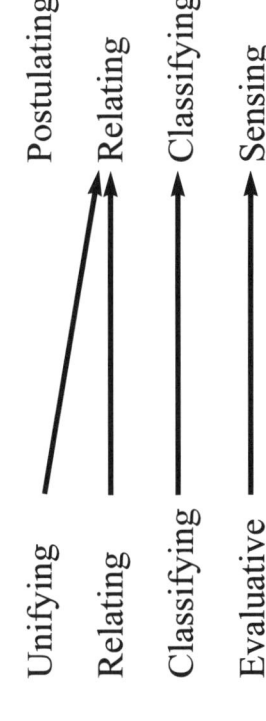

Illustration 3

Circular Process

1 ⟷ 2 ⟷ 3

Levels ⟷ Types ⟷ Orders

3   2   1

(Analysis) ⟷ (Evaluation/ ⟷ (Examination)
Diagnosis)

It is a circular process, whereby the orders examine and types diagnose, evaluate and analyze, and levels analyze. Types undergo a revision and the process continues.

Illustration 4

A Look at the Notion of Leadership with Types and Levels

LEVELS (differences in degree/meaning change but definition remains the same)

Emphasis: Differences in Degree

TYPES (differences in kind/meanings and definitions change)

Emphasis: Differences in Kind

1. One Leader Definition
   Evaluative: Not chosen—not elected, inherited.

2. One Leader Definition—unquestioned.
   Classifying: different degrees—still one leader but good or bad. No Shades of grey. Chosen or elected.
   Meaning Change—Not Definition

3. Relating: Feedback in Leadership. Formal—Definition the same, but meaning changes. Still one leader but involves others—limited and mechanical.

4. Unifying: Leadership with not over. Formal definition the same but meanings change: Integration, but never postulation, still one leader but unlimited participation.

1. Sensing
   Reactive to leadership/charismatic/one-way leadership—all downward

2. Classifying: different kind of determination/formal or informal. Leadership up or down/right or wrong. Rigid logical leadership. Top/bottom definition and meaning change—two way leadership either bottom or top.
   Active/Definiton change from sensing.

3. Relating: Several kinds of leadership, up and down, horizontal and vertical, mechanical, crisscross, informal and formal. Interactive/definition change from classifying.
   Many leaders—circular. This part of relating applies to unifying level.

4. Postulating: the loss of definition of the concept of leadership. The word leadership disappears—this is transformation. (transactive). Definition change—paradigm shift.

NOTE: With levels—the word leadership is used at each level and each level retains the same definition even when meanings change.

NOTE: With types—the word leadership disappears with the (postulating) type.

Illustration 5

An Integrating Picture

ORDERS	TYPES—(Evaluating)	LEVELS—(Meticulous Analysis of types and orders)
1. Event	Sensing (Reaction) Homosexuality—Behavioral Inference i.e., What it looks like based on intensional thinking.	Level—evaluative Decides the kind of *reaction* to homosexuality Evaluative Classifying Relating Unifying
2. First-order Experience	Classifying—type (Action) (Homosexuality/bi-sexuality) Definition change Concrete categories	Level—classifying Decides the kind of homosexuality Evaluative Classifying Relating Unifying
3. Description	Relating—type (Interaction) (Sexuality) Definition change General	Level—relating Decides the kind of sexuality, Classifying, Relating, Unifying, Evaluative
4. Label:	Postulating—type (Transaction) Symbol engaged/word no longer used Definition change Very abstract—not concrete A Transformation/Tentative abductive. Cannot be analyzed with levels.	Level—unifying Decides the kind of Classifying, Relating, Unifying and Evaluative. Postulating is exempt from levels because of the definition change. Levels do not examine the postulating type.

How to read this illustration: Types evaluate the particular order, and levels analyze the mode of each order and the character of each type, except the postulating type. The above is just to illustrate how the process works.

Dr. William J. Williams

The illustration points out how the notion of "leadership" should be viewed and the differences between the notion as viewed by levels and types.

1. There is an indication of where levels and orders fit within types; but,
2. It is not indicated how levels can analyze once a selection is made. We will do it now.

Suppose the one-way "leadership" is the selection. The notion of one-way leadership can be of the sensing or classifying types, depending upon the definition used. Then, levels are inserted to analyze one way type leadership. We merely insert levels in order to meticulously and rigorously analyze the kind of one way leadership. If the one way leadership embraces compromise or a feedback mechanism to implement the leadership philosophy, that would be the relating level. To repeat: The type, which may be sensing or classifying, does not change, however—the level does. If it is solely charismatic leadership and always at the top or inherited, as in kingship, and so on, it is at the sensing stage (level). If there is a selection process and the bottom leadership can become the top leadership, it is at the classifying level. If it encourages information from the bottom, it is an interactive-relating level. If it embraces many levels within the type it becomes a unifying level, but still remains one decision—realizing as the typing. This is how levels enable us to interpret meticulously within a particular type.

Now, let's focus on all of the processes of abstracting as an integrated unit and simultaneously examine a substantive subject graphically; in this case homosexuality.

If one concludes, for example, that the type is sensing, then the use of levels would pinpoint the kind of sensing and other elements that may be within the overall typed "classification." The meticulous analysis of each type and order enables us to identify, in a rigorous fashion, the weights, values, and specifics of types and orders, which in turn enables us to make that huge and necessary distinction between propositions and propositional functions.

For example, let's continue with the discussion started under orders in which we referred to the way we approach questions on affirmative action. In some cases, we refer to it as reverse discrimination. This is also a third order, an order after the descriptive order. We indulge in dead-level abstracting when we use reverse. Reverse, by definition, is

New Thinking For A New Millennium

incorrect. One discrimination is not the same as another. They are defined differently and have different reasons for existence. However, once we call it reverse, we assume sameness. We are again confusing orders. Thus, the subject is lost, because we have moved the discussion to a labeling order. The focus of the discussion is directed improperly.

In short, the second kind of discrimination is different from the first. Once we put them in the same category, those differences are lost and we have an inappropriate discussion. We have confused the orders of abstraction and levels of abstracting. In terms of levels, the first kind of discrimination would be at the classifying level, but the second would be at the relating level (the one we call reverse). However, both would be the classifying type. The first discrimination was designed to ban minorities. The one called reverse discrimination was designed to include minorities, which is in keeping with effective time-binding. The time-binding mission is to integrate and improve social, economic, and political relations, thus making the nation a better place in which to live. The time-binding missions are different. The first discrimination is about segregation and the so-called "reverse" is about integration. They are of different orders and, therefore, we should not disqualify the second unless we change the type. That would require an elimination of both. That change would require a different set of methods. It would be too hard to dismiss the second unless the new methods would enable us to rectify what the first has wrought.

Theoretically, those who oppose affirmative action are correct, but they are practically incorrect. The opponents maintain that we cannot stop racism by practicing racism, although the racisms are on two different levels of abstracting. It does, however, change the practical consequences of the racism it is designed to manage. It does not, however, eliminate racism. The question is: what is the best way of eliminating racism? Is it moving to a different stage of thinking and a different type of abstracting? Yes, that's the ideal way. We are stuck, however, with a practical world in which that idealism does not work to change the circumstances. For example, if we had not had the bus boycott in Montgomery, segregation might still be around. The proponents of segregation maintained that it was not about changing laws, but about changing the hearts of people. We changed the laws, which was practical. The theoretical situations of hearts still exist. That may or may not change. Likewise, in the case of affirmative action, it brings about a practical solution, which to a large extent leaves untouched the theoretical dynamics of racism in the broader sense.

Dr. William J. Williams

Then, which method is better? Is it the use of levels of abstracting to address the practical aspects, or the use of types of abstracting to address the theoretical aspects? Which will lead us to our ultimate goals? The answer is both. We must deal with the practical, put a tentative "tag" on it, and have as a long-range objective the theoretical as it pertains to types of abstracting. If we focus only on the theoretical, the practical lives of individuals will continue to be intolerable and ultimately lead to disaster. The ideal state of affairs that would make affirmative action unnecessary does not exist. We live in a political, mechanical world that calls for measures that hug the moving realities of a system that denies entry and equity to minorities and women. It is a delicate balance.

The same process can enable us to understand many of our situations, as in the fraud case involving ABC and the grocery store chain. The principle here is to understand the dynamics of the levels of abstracting regarding the notion of fraud. This principle was illustrated on *Nightline*. The television show comprised of a senior executive from the show and lawyers and representatives from Food Lion, Inc. discussing whether or not the jury verdict against ABC in a lawsuit brought by Food Lion was justified. The jury verdict was based on the notion that ABC had committed fraud when they brought in hidden cameras to expose unsanitary meat handling. The discussion revolved around whether or not ABC's efforts to expose fraud were justified. Senator Alan Simpson said fraud is fraud. Well, this is dead-level abstracting, and fraud is not fraud. Fraud to expose fraud is a different kind of fraud, just as racism to eliminate a certain kind of racism is a different kind of racism—or saying never about never is legitimate, or always avoid always. If this structural method had been used to dissect, the chances of a resolution and understanding between the groups may have been embraced. Nobody there was able to insert the notion of levels of abstracting, which would have put the discussion in perspective and enabled the communication process to become more effective. With levels of abstracting, we bend the ultimate principle to achieve a modicum of justice, leaving the ultimate principle intact to be addressed by stages and types of abstracting. We indulge in the confusing of levels of abstracting daily in high-level policy processes and in our personal lives. Thus, our decision making is hampered. Epistemologically, the verb "to be" is the culprit, because it directs our thinking into dead-level abstracting; examples are pigs are pigs, a man

New Thinking For A New Millennium

is a man, a doctor is a doctor, a crook is a crook, a cop is a cop. It emphasizes sameness.

Chapter Nine

The Style

A part of the "integration" process is style. The style is determined by the kind of equation, worldview, or mindset one brings to the application. The equation (style) is evaluated with types and levels of abstracting. We need to determine what elements are necessary to successfully implement the process that will be necessary for rigorous, meticulous, and qualitative analysis. Styles of abstracting have to do with the broader aspects of the subject. In a general and broad sense, the style is determined by values, genetic makeup, the culture and, in a secondary sense, the language and one's professional worldview. Style, buttressed by a methodology described with the notions of levels and of types of abstracting, appears to be the most powerful at this time. Styles of abstracting serve as the theoretical overarching process.

In order to identify a style, there must be a consciousness of orders, of abstracting levels, and types of abstracting. It is all one holistic circular process being analytically separated for the purpose of graphically depicting, in an artistic fashion, a connection that is synthetic, nonlinear. and nonelementalistic. The formulation is a crude map of the territory, it is verbal. It is but a rough application of the actual events. The rules that govern the use of the processes also govern the design and designer of the processes. In short, what I say about this process and the particular type explanation may be accurate, but not totally adequate. However, because of this process, we did introduce, unlike some other methods, some adequacy as well as accuracy. Therefore, the process becomes automatically self-reflexive and self-revising. The nonlinear approach and attitude provides the direction. The key to the effective use of this style and utilization of it on both a theoretical (as a theoretician) and practitioner "level" (as a professional) is the understanding and internalizing of the orders of abstraction and

New Thinking For A New Millennium

levels and styles of abstracting. With this understanding and internalizing of orders, levels, and types of abstracting, adequate evaluation and meticulous analysis will occur. However, the lack of an in-depth understanding will not foreclose some accuracy and a modicum of adequacy from occuring. The key terms here are accuracy and adequacy! The style with which we abstract is determined by a myriad of factors, including our values, environment, cultural upbringing, semantic transactions, and so on. These all lead to a stylistic and individualized approach to any situation. To understand the processes of abstracting, we must approach them as a semantic transactions. The elements of the semantic transactor are: *past, present, future, electrochemical, feelings, thinking, muscular activity and, in general, the environment.* The environment does not simply refer to physical surroundings, but to everything that influences our daily activities. The semantic transaction is a transaction that is determined by the actual situation—the outside event, the word that is spoken, the thought that occurs, the hope that emerges, and what it means to the individual at a given moment (Bois 1996).

We are aware that we are related to all things in the world, with a structure that distinguishes us from the rest of the world. The structure has been built, over time, as our transactions were internalized and various inputs ingested.

Transactions are determined by the meaning a situation has for the individual. Moreover, the value we assign to a situation depends on the structure of valuations we have internalized. In this respect, statements we make on the environment external to us are actually statements we make on the environment internal to us. We copy through our transactions—our conditions or statess—so that general remarks to the world are self-commentary and observations become self-diagnosis. Hence, to determine how we see and inquire about the world is to see how we think. To see how we structure our way of knowing the world is to see the structure within us.

The style outlined is essential for the theoretician and practitioner. The practitioner who also becomes a good theoretician, in this sense, becomes a more effective practitioner. This separates the true professional practitioner from the "professional" practitioner. I will not elaborate on this because it would take us too far afield, except to say in the words of Kurt Lewin, "a truly great practitioner is a great theoretician" who has of course, focused on proper theoretical concerns. The key term here is proper.

Epilogue

A theory may be good, but if the wrong methodological approach is used to implement it, the theory will not work. For example, when Abraham Maslow said in his *Farther Reaches of Human Nature* that he would use the scientific method to achieve his stage of self-actualizing and transcendence, he was advocating a methodology that did not fit.

Likewise, there are some good theories without methodological processes. In these instances, it is up to us to develop, find, and/or invent appropriate methodologies to make them applicable. For example, in Follette's *Creative Experience,* the ideas of creative unity and the law of the situation were advanced. However, there was nothing to tell us how to implement this. Hopefully, the methods introduced in this book will enable us to identify the laws of the situation and bring about creative unity. Without the appropriate methodologies, finding the law of the situation and self-actualization may be impossible.

A common mistake we make is trying to use quantitative methodologies to understand and implement qualitative activities. They are not mutually exclusive. However, how they fit together is important. It's not always either/or. The quantitative part can be used, but not at certain "levels." I was "flipping" television channels one night and heard Ted Turner, the chairman and CEO of Turner Broadcasting, Inc., making a speech to the Howard University School of Journalism. He said something that I agreed with, that the important thing is to know "how to think." The second thing he said was that one had to be lucky. I agree with both, but because the latter is mystical, I cannot deal with it in applications. Einstein said the same thing—that "the only thing important to teach is how to think"—but neither said how. We then not only need the admonition, but need to know how to go about doing it—a prescription with a method. This treatise I am presenting speaks not only about the admonition, but about how and what the ingredients ought to be to achieve the goal of thinking.

I once called my approach nondisciplinary instead of interdisciplinary, and/or multidisciplinary. A friend of mine, Dr. Robert Biller, wrote me a note indicating that he thought the term was inappropriate. The use of the term nondisciplinary was intended to separate out a process that did not belong to any particular discipline. In other words, I considered the process I was championing to be on a different order and stage of abstracting. To remain with interdisciplinary and multidisciplinary would have put them on the same level. Secondly, I considered my approach more of a container than a content. Thirdly, I thought it best to be "nondisciplinary," since it might be easier to remember when counterpoised against the notions of multidisciplinary and interdisciplinary. I thought about Dr. Biller's criticism and decided for several reasons to substitute the phrase epistemic focus, epistemics because it is the practical application of epistemological assumptions. Therefore, I am splitting the difference and authorizing the reader to use nondisciplinary, or epistemic focus, or both.

Glossary of Terms

abduction: A term first used by Charles S. Pierce in 1867 to show a logical sequence to intuitive thinking; a process that has natural affinity for understanding events. It precedes hypotheses and the other methods of inquiry. It is a mindset. It is an all-embracing method incorporating all others.

absolute statement: A statement without flexibility. It is fixed thinking with no shades of gray.

abstracting: A process featuring notions about how we think and the analysis and evolving out of that thinking. A circular process introduced by Arthur Korzybski.

aggregates: Mass of separate things pinned together. Collective group.

allness: Narrow thinking, generalizations.

applied epistemology: A phrase coined by Felix Roethlisberger to enable the structuring, selection, invention and application of basic knowledge.

Aristotelianism: A style of thinking, utilizing Aristotle's method of inquiry. Namely, deductive method featuring syllogistic reasoning, and either/or thinking strict categories.

binary concept: Idea of having two variables, two components, or two possible choices.

classifying stage: The second stage of the epistemological profile utilizing early classical Greek thought and Aristotle's methodology.

conceptualization: The process of imagining and identifying areas of thought symbolically.

conditionality: Dependent, not absolute, and limited by surroundings.

New Thinking For A New Millennium

constructs: Groups of words in phrases, perceptions or thoughts, or emerging concepts.

contextualism: Holistic thinking—wholeness, nonfragmentation.

contradictories: (1) A term that exactly negates another; (2) A proposition so related to a second that either must be false if one is true. Values assigned.

contraries: Framed like contradictories, but having no assigned specific values.

creative loop: A methodology designed by Dr. J. Samuel Bois for the purpose of making the abductive process practical and useable.

deduction: Designation for Aristotelian logic, using the syllogism as a methodology. Process of reasoning using a general principle that is accepted as a truth and reaching a conclusion based on preassumed "truth."

differentiation: The act or process of making a distinction or choice.

ebonics: A language.

elementalism: Separate unity concepts, fragmentation.

epistemic system: A practical-theoretical system of thought emphasizing applied epistemology, the episteme, the process of abduction, general semantics epistemology, and the application of other basic knowledge.

epistemological profile: An instrument invented by the French philosopher Gaston Bachelard, designed to aid us in analyzing the deeper structures of our "thought-combining" theory and practice.

epistemology: Philosophy that deals with origins, natures, and limits of knowledge—how and why we think as we do, how our knowledge and thinking are invented and developed, and how and why we think what we think.

formism: A root metaphor emphasizing static thinking.

fragmentation: The opposite of wholeness and holism. A partial or piecemeal approach to thinking. Disconnectedness and isolated and incomplete ways of thinking.

fusion: A blend, or coalition—combining schools of thought. A communion of ideas or thinking processes.

Dr. William J. Williams

Gestalt: A form of psychology emphasizing that a whole may be more than the sum of its parts. The parts are often modified by their relationship to the whole and to each other.

holism: Theory based on presumed importance and tendency of nature to produce wholeness.

homeostatic: Maintaining internal equilibrium.

Hopi: Refers to the language structure of Pueblo Indian tribe of northern Arizona.

horizontal focus: Involving one stage of thinking—lateral focus.

induction: Idea introduced by Sir Francis Bacon. It is in line with our positivistic thinking and the scientific method. It is also used in analytical research. Method used to form a general rule or principle by collecting many cases to find out by experimentation what is common to all.

integration: Arrangement or combination of ideas and responses into a harmonious unit or whole. A syndrome for the third type of abstracting and third level of abstracting.

interaction: A term coined from classical physics denoting cause and effect (stimulus-response), and push and pull physics. Separate entities influencing and acting upon each other with cause and effect. A symbol for the third type of abstracting and third level.

interdisciplinary: Relationship between differing and varied fields of study.

invariance: Unchanging, constant, fixed form of perception.

is of identity: Absolute statement with no scope for variables or questions. Emphasis is on finality and the definite rather than inquiry and the infinite.

is of predication: Assertion or affirmation about or of a subject.

language: The symbolic process.

levels: Differences in degree and not kind.

logical postivism: An attempt to link facts and values in a systematic way. Symbolic logic is used and linguistic problems of meaning are emphasized.

New Thinking For A New Millennium

mechanisitc mode: Seventeenth-century thinking. A part of the relating stage of the epistemological profile and the second conceptual revolution. A format for achieving the third type of abstracting.

multidisciplinlary: Involving many branches of learning.

multiordinality: A system used to order the process of abstracting; that is, something can have different meanings at different levels of abstracting without abandoning the original definition. Moving of terms, subjects, and ideas from one level to another without definition change. Used only with levels of abstracting.

Newtonian: A philosophy designed to characterize the scientific method and used to define the third type of abstracting and level of abstracting.

orders: A term used to order the abstracting process.

ordinal aspects: Ordered or positioned in a series.

organicism: Having self-contained and automatic responses. Connected parts similar to the biological mental model.

paradigms: Thoughts and patterns of behavior transforming our ways of functioning: A difference in kind, not degree; a difference that makes a difference a difference.

positivism: Philosophical system recognizing only positive facts and the visible. A rejection of metaphysics. Free of values, "objective."

postulating stage: The fourth stage of the epistemological profile in which things are tentative and flexible. The stage of relativity and modern science (transactional as opposed to interactive).

postulation: Fundamental principle, not taking for granted assumptions without proof and holding ideas tentative and flexible.

predication: Assertion or affirmation as truth.

process of abstracting: The natural process of our thinking and nervous system invented by Alfred Korzybski; the major distinction between plants, animals, and humans.

qualitative: Concerned with quality, as opposed to quantitative.

quantitative: Measure or measurable, and concerned with amount, portion, or size. Quality not necessarily emphasized; counting.

quantum: Probability, uncertainty, et cetera—cause-effect rejection, abductive.

Dr. William J. Williams

reaction: An action in response to some influence or force.

relating stage: The third stage of the epistemological profile, represents the thinking of the seventeenth century. It embraces classical physics, positivism, logical positivism, scientific method and inductive reasoning: The second conceptual revolution.

self-reflexive: Introducing oneself into the process and including a map of the map into infinity.

semantic: Relating to the meaning of language. Connotation of words.

semantic transaction: A way of using the seven elements jointly, of the semantic transaction to holistically function.

sensing stage: The first stage of the epistemological profile (pre-Grecian and pre-Aristotelian).

situation: A substitution, symbolically and semantically, for the term or problem.

structural approach: Finding a symbolic process that has a meaningful correspondence to the structure of this world.

syllogistic reasoning: Aristotelian method.

symbolic process: The language system we use.

synthesizing: Bringing together seemingly unrelated instances.

theory of logical types: A theory proposed by Bertrand Russell to free us from the Aristotelian vicious circle fallacy and static thinking.

time-binding: A term used by Alfred Korzybski. The major distinction between plants, humans, and animals. The capacity to make symbols and abstractions and pass on knowledge from one generation to another. The time-binding capacity. The mindset behind his thinking (sane, unsane, and insane).

"to be:" Identity. The verb "to be" and its harmfulness to human functioning.

transaction: As opposed to interactions coined by Arthur Bentley to represent a process that speaks of fusion and being holistically connected.

transformation: A process theoretically more open to the natural process of human development. It has as its undergirding thought process; the theory of dissipative and functioning. A semantic or epistemic jump. A difference that makes a difference a difference.

New Thinking For A New Millennium

Fourth type of abstracting and fifth stage of the epistemological profile.

translation: Interpretation of meaning in plainer words. Infer or declare significance.

types: Differences in kinds of abstracting. Types.

undergirding: Strengthening and making secure from underneath.

underpinning: Deep underneath process. Microscopic and submicroscopic.

WIGO: What is going on.

References

Bachelard, Gaston. 1940. *The Philosophy of No.* New York: Orion Press. Translated Grossman Publishers, 1968.

Bentley, Arthur. 1939. *Linguistic Analysis of Mathematics.* Bloomington: Principia Press.

Bentley, Arthur. 1949. *Knowing and the Known.* Boston: Beacon Press.

Bohm, David. 1949. *Fragmentation and Wholeness.* Israel: Van Leer: Jerusalem Foundation.

Bois, J. Samuel. 1996. *The Art of Awareness.* Santa Monica, Calif.: Continuum Press.

Boulding, Kenneth. 1956. *The Image.* Ann Arbor: University of Michigan Press.

Bridgeman, Percy. 1966. *The Way Things Are.* Cambridge: Harvard University Press.

Carroll, John B., ed. 1962. *Language, Thought and Reality: Selected Writings of Benjamin Whorf.* Cambridge, Mass.: The M.I.T. Press.

Devlin, Keith. 1997. *Goodbye Descartes.* New York: John Wiley and Sons.

Devlin, Keith. 1996. *Language at Work.* Cambridge: Cambridge University Press.

Ellis, Dr. Albert. 1975. *A New Guide to Rational Living.* North Hollywood, Calif.: Wilshire Book Company.

Follette, Mary Parker. 1924. *Creative Experience.* New York: Longmans Green and Co.

Fox, Elliot M. and L. Urwick. 1977. "Dynamic Administration." *The Collected Papers of Mary Parker Follette*. New York: Hippocrene Books.

International Society For General Semantics. Et cetera: *Review of General Semantics*. Concord, Calif.: International Society For General Semantics.

Korzybski, Alfred. 1933. *Science and Sanity*. Lakeville, CT:

Kosko, Bart. 1993. *Fuzzy Thinking*. New York: Hyperion.

Maslow, Abraham. 1973. *Farther Reaches of Human Nature*. New York: Viking Press.

Pepper, Stephen. 1970. *World Hypotheses*. Berkeley, Calif.: University of California Press.

Russell, Bertrand. 1910. *Principia Mathematica*. London: Cambridge University Press.

Weinberg, Harry. 1955. *Levels of Knowing and Existence*. New York: Harper and Row.

Whorf, Benjamin Lee. See Carroll, John B.

Williams, William J. 1976. *Uncommon Sense and Dimensional Awareness*. Los Angeles: University Publishers.

Williams, William J. 1971. *General Semantics and the Social Sciences*. New York: Philosophical Library.

Williams, William J. 1985. *The Miracle of Abduction*. Los Angeles: Epistemic Institute Press.

Williams, William J. 1978. *Semantic Behavior and Decision Making*. Ann Arbor: Monograph Publishing.

Index

A New Guide to Rational Living, 19
ABC, 81
abduction, 15, 55
abductive process, xvii
absolute, 7
   language, 12
   statement, 71
   truth, 25
absoluteness, 21
abstracting, xvii, xviii
   classifying (See classifying abstracting)
   consciousness of, xviii
   consciousness, 29
   dead level, 61
   language, 11
   levels, 59
   non-consciousness of,
   notion of, 45
   objective, 63
   orders, 45, 63
   process, xvii, xviii, 46
   processes, 22
   relating, 61
   stages, 56
   styles, 83
   types, 53, 55
   unifying, 64
abstraction, 45
   first-order, 45
   mathematical, 26
   orders, 46
accurate, 11, 84
adequate, 11, 84
affirmative action, 50, 80
Age of Logical Positivism,
aggregates, 10
   law of, 3
   theory, 10
alcohol prohibition analogy,
ambiguious, 49
analysis, 71
   levels, 11
   methodological, 9
   meticulous, 78
   meticulous qualitative rigorous, 78
   qualitative, 9 ,78
   qualitative rigorous, 78
   quantitative, 78
   rigorous, 78
analytical, xv
   process, xx
   theory, 23
   thinking,
   animal, 34
   analogue, 23

analogy, 25
experimentation, 24
model, 26
animalistic categorizing, 61
animistic, 22
abstracting, 30
Anti-thesis Synthesis and Back to Thesis, 27
Aristotelian, 31, 73
  logic, 31
  philosophy, thinking, 73
Aristotle, 37
Arnold, Matthew, 33
art of at oneness, 39
Art of Awareness, 87
atomistic view, 29
awareness,
  of language, ix

Bachelard Gaston, 27
Bacon, 55, 73
balance, 8
balance of power, 9
balances and checks, 23
barber analogy, 23, 49
behavior,
Bentley, Arthur, xvi, 13
Biller, Dr. Robert, 86
binary, 17
biological, 34-35
  animal model, 23
  cell model, 23
  plant model, 24
  thinking process, x
biology, 27
blank slate, 31
Bohm, David, 29
Bois, J. Samuel, 29
Boulding, Kenneth, 29, 73

branches of government, ix
Bridgeman, Percy, 29
Burke, Edmund, 26
buzz words, 18

calculus, 2
  language, 7
  notion ,7
cardinal aspects, 1
Cartesian thinking, xvi
causality, 54
cell model, 27
checks and balances, 6, 33
chicken and egg analogy, 3, 4
chlorophyll, 25
circular, 76
  process, 7, 8, 42
  responses, 42
circularity, 12
  natural, 13
  of the brain, 13
circulatory systems (See Human)
classifying, 61
  abstracting, 10, 23, 53, 59
  levels, 10
  logical, 59, 60, 62
  objective, 54
  strict, 62, 63
  types, 53, 54
clockwork, 22, 32
mechanical analogy, 33
mechanistic metaphor, 26
metaphor, 27, 29, 30
model, 27
structure, 29
co-dependency, 59
commandment, law of, 20
common sense, 10
commonality, 39, 60
communication, 41

complexification, 30, 35
compromise, 59
concept of group, 21
conceptual, 27
   notion, 27
   process, 67
   revolutions, 69
Conceptual Revolutions, 73
conceptualization, 8, 31
conditionality, 28
conflict, 11, 18
connectedness, 9
consciousness,
   of abstracting, xviii, 48
construction theory, x
constructs, 23, 29
container, 56
content, 56
contextual,
   analogy, 29
   metaphor, 40
   process, 39
   root metaphor, 28
contextualism, 36, 37
contradictory, 7
contrary, 7
conversion process,
Copernicus, 62
correspondence, 10, 11
   natural, 9
   primary, 11
   structural, 13, 14
   structural similarity, 10
   structure, x
   symbolic, x
   the how-secondary, 10
   the what primary, 9
   theory of, 7
creative experience, 85
creativity, 59

cybernetics, 23, 31

Darwin, Charles, 36
dead level (See abstracting-dead level)
deduction, 23
deductive, 61
   process, 45
   reasoning, 61
   definition, 20
Deist, 26
dependency, 26
dependent, 27
   variable, 46
Descartes, 55, 59
description, 28
descriptive order, 59
Devlin, Keith, xx
diagnostic process, 76
dictionary definition, 56
differences, 61
   in degree, 72
   in kind, 9, 53
   meaning, 56
differentiation, 23, 32
digestive system (See human)
discrimination, 80
domination, 67
dynamic, 29
   administration, 68
   function, 60
   moving structure, 29
   process, 18
   structure,
dynamics, 38
   Galilean, 37
   Newtonian, 38
dysfunction, 24

East and West, 23, 27
ebonics, xxiii

E-choice, 22
Einstein, 70
  relativity, 70
  theory,
Einsteinian, 6
either/or, 68
electrical theory, 29
electrochemical, 39
electromagnetism, 29
elementalism, 9, 18
Ellis, Dr. Albert, 19
emergence, xviii, 27, 29
Emerson, 37
empirical, 57
  world,
epicycles, 28
Epistemic Focus, 79
epistemics, x, 69
epistemological,
  background, 9, 23
  focus, 13
  inquiry method, 71
  perspective, 24
  process, 14
  profile, 30
  undergirding, 11
  underpinnings, 50, 73
epistemology,
E-prime, 19
evaluating, 75
  levels, 10
  procedure, 46
  reaction, 53
  types, 72
evaluation, 23, 59, 60
event, 9, 10, 25
  world of (See world of events)
evolution theory, 27
excluded middle, viii
  law of,

Farther Reaches of Human Nature, 85
feedback, 46
feminism, 61
first-order,
  abstraction, 12
  experience, 48
flow-charts, 37, 41
fluoride, 69
Follette, Mary Parker, 70, 85
formism, 30
formistic, xviii, 26
  framework model, 31
  model, 39
  thinking, 35
fragmentation, 6, 26, 27
Fragmentation and Wholeness, 29
framework, xxi
  formistic model, 26
  levels, 27
  model, 28
  new, xx, 8
  static, 39
  system, 37
fraud, 76
function, 19, 23, 32
  notion of, 7
  theory of, 3
fusion, 67
Fuzzy Thinking, 1, 15

Galilean dynamics, 32
Galileo, 60
Gandhi, 70, 71
gay (See homosexuality)
geometry, 2
glossary of terms, 87
Goodbye Descartes, xxi
government, 6
  branches of, 6

system of, 5
treaties of, 33
grammar, 45
grammatical, 48
  process, 48
  proposition, 46
  structure, 20
gravitation, 9
  notion of, 9
  theory of universal, 27
group, 9
  concept of, 9
  notion of, 10
guide for knowing and naming, 7

harmony, 29
Hawking, Stephen, ix
heart transplant analogy, 60
Hegel, George Wilhelm Frederick, 34
Heisenberg, 16
heterosexual, 60
holistic, 83
  inquiry methods, 9, 19
homeostatic, 25, 36
homosexuality, 54, 56, 72
honesty, 59
Hopi, xxiv
horizontal, 9
  focus, 5
how, 9
  the how-secondary, 9
human, 36
  analogue, 26
  behavior, 37
  circulatory system, 27
  digestive system, 27
  function, 13
  metaphor, 37
  mind, 4

model, 29
nervous system. (See nervous system)
relational language, 1
reproductive system, 29
self-reflexive, 31
sexuality, 56
Hume, David, 33

identification, 1
identity law of, 46
illegitimate totality, 4
illogic, xx
Image, The, 39
implementation, 2, 7
independent variables, 7
induction, 32
infinity, iv
inquiry, vi
  epistemological, 69
  methods, 27
  methods holistic, 5
insight, 27, 31
integration, xx, 68
  conflict, 68
  process, 71
  thought, 78
interaction, 13, 68
interactive process, 71
interconnectedness, 16
interdependency, 29
interdisciplinary, 26
interpretation, 41
interrelatedness, 29
invariance, 11
irrational number, 2
is of identification, 3
is of identity, 2, 19, 22
is of predication, 20
isolationism, 29

Kepler, 60
knowing and naming, 23
  epistemological background, 23
  epistemological perspective, 23
knowing and the known, 13
knowledge synthesizing of,
Koppel Ted, 84
Korzybski Alfred, 45, 46
Kosko Bart, 4, 16

l'homme Machine, 32
La Meetre, 33
language, 9, 10, 12
  absolute, 20
  abstracting, 4
  awareness of, xi
  calculus, 8
  common sense, 8
  ebonics, xi
  Hopi, 19
  intricacies of, xviii
  mathematical, 3
  mathematics, 9, 12
  nonidentity, 8
  notion of, 9
  old, 10
  ordinary, 11
  relational, 21
  relational human, 1
  structure, 1, 9, 20
  subject predicate, 20
Language At Work, xxi
Language Thought and Reality, 19
law of,
  aggregates, 10
  commandment, 21
  excluded middle, 47
  identity, 48
  noncontradiction, 42, 48
  nonidentity, 47

permanency, 20, 48
situation, 68
leadership, 77, 79
legitimate totality, 14
lemon analogy, 27
levels,
  abstracting (See abstracting-levels)
  analysis (See analysis levels)
  classifying (See classifying-levels)
  evaluating (See evaluating levels)
  framework, 24
  metaphoric, 29
  primitive, 61
  relating (See relating-levels)
  thinking, 63
  unifying (See unifying levels)
Levels of Knowing and Existence, 49
Lewin Kurt, 84
linear,
  logic, 9, 11
  mathematics, 3
  notion of, 9
  structure, 71
Linguistic Analysis of Mathematics and Knowing and the Known, xvi
local causes, theory, 7
Locke John, 33
logic, 20
  Aristotelian, 19, 23
  fixed, 61
  linear, 8
  non-Aristotelian, 33
Logical Positivism, 62
  Age of, 62
  world of, 54

Los Angeles Times, x
machine model, 63
macroscopic, 65
Man a Machine, 27
map, 59
  objective reality, 65
map-territory, 45, 46, 59
Maslow, 85
mathematics, 42
  abstraction, 9, 10, 11, 15
  calculus, 11
  geometry, 11
  language, 12
  linear, 16
  new, 20
  nonlinear, 19
  structure, 16
  symbols, 9
meaning, 56
  change, 56
  new,
  variable, 10
measure, 29, 31
  inner, 26, 32
  inward, 29
  notion of, 38
mechanical, 6
  clockwork analogy, 25
  logical, 29
  metaphor, 35
  method, 3
  model, 36
  process, 31
  structure, 6, 33
  system, 7
  theory of matter, 28
  thinking, 37
mechanics quantum, 27
mechanism, 32
mechanistic, 38
mechanistic metaphor, 31
mederi, 28
mediation, 39
Mental Models, 40
metamorphosis, 6
metaphor, 38, 39, 41
  contextual, 39
  human, 37
  literal, 39
  mechanical, 37
  mechanistic, 33
  organicism, 39
  root (See root metaphor)
metaphoric, 31
  levels, 31
  vehicles, 32
methodological, 36
  analysis, 20, 59
  focus, 39, 41
  process, 72
  stages, 29
methodology, 75
meticulous, 42
  analysis, 6
  qualitative rigorous analysis, 45
  rigorous,
  rigorous analysis, 58
  rigorous qualitative, 19, 42
microscopes, 58
microscopic, 7
mindset, 29, 72
minorities,
moderation, 51
Montgomery, bus boycott, 80
motion of the planets, 25
motivation, 39
multidisciplinary, 59
multiordinality, 3, 59
multiplier theory, 29

natural,
  biological thinking process, 34-35
  circularity, 10
  correspondence, 9
  functioning, 6, 52
  orders, 5
  processes, 12
  science, 26
  structure, 9
  survival order of the nervous system, 47
natural functioning,
  nervous system,
nervous system, 10
  autonomic, 35
  functioning, 40
  natural functioning, 11
  natural survival order, 49
  structure, 49
Newton, 25, 33, 73
Newtonian, 6, 25
  dynamics, 29
  physics, 31
  theory, 32
non-Aristotelian, 9
  logic, 9
non-consciousness of abstracting, 26
noncontent, 10
noncontradiction law of, xviii
non-disciplinary, 86
nonelementalism, 9
nonfragmentation, 9
nonidentity, 92
  law of, 46
  theory, 19, 46
nonlinear, 16, 19
nonlogical, 1
non-Newtonian, 36

nonreferential, 12
nonself-subsistent, 7
nonstatic, 32
non-subject-verb-object, 9
non-subject-verb-predicate, 11
nonverbal map, 47
notion of,
  abstracting, 9
  calculus, 10
  conceptual, 11
  function, 7
  gravitation, 7
  group, 8
  invariance, 6, 20
  language, 10
  linear, 9
  measure, 27

objectification, 29
objective,
  abstracting, 59
  classifying, 60
  step, 19
objectivity, 42
old,
  grammar, 47
  language, 6
  science, 18
  thinking, 42
oneness, 27
orders, 48, 68
  abstraction (See abstraction orders)
organic, 8
organicism, 35
  root metaphor, 35
organimistic, 35
  methods, 39
  thinking, 26
organismic semantic reaction, 23

Orient (See East and West)

paradigms, 77
participation, 23, 29
Pepper, Stephen, 39
permanence, 31
permanency,
  law of, 53
perspective,
phenomenology,
philosophy, 28
  Aristotelian, 35
photosynthesis, 36
physics, 9
  Newtonian,
  quantum,
Pierce, Charles,
Planck, Max, 56
plant model, 39, 40
Plato, 31
positivistic, 27
postulation, 19
  principle of, 69
  type, 56
power,
  balance of, 19
  over, 72
  with, 73
practitioner, 77
pre-Aristotelian, 33
pre-rationality thinking, 71
Principia Mathematica, 48
principle of linguistic relativity, 22
probability, 19
  theory, 20
process,
  abstracting (See abstracting-process)
  analytical, 46

circular, 59
conceptual, 67
contextual, 67
deductive, 44
diagnostic, 49
division, 28
dynamic, 26
epistemological, 29
grammatical,
  inquiry, 76
integration, 72
interactive, 71
internalizing, 67
mechanical, 27
methodological, 29
overarching, 77
principle of, 42
qualitative, 75
selection, 72
self-connecting,
  structural, 70
submicroscopic, 47
thinking, 24
undergirding, 9
underlying,
processes, 43
  abstracting (See abstracting-processes)
prohibition of alcohol analogy,
proposition, 47
  grammatical, 21
propositional function, 6, 47, 48
Ptolemaic, 23

qualitative, 5
  analysis, 5
  formulation, 39
  method, 34
  process, 41
  rigorous, 46

rigorous analysis, 47
rigorous meticulous, 38
rigorous meticulous analysis, 38
rigorous process,
quantitative, 60
   analysis, 9
   methodology, 29, 32
quantum, 27, 29
   mechanics, 1
   physics, 14
quarks, 18
quota, 48

racism, 59, 67
reaction, 56
   organismic semantic, 23
   primitive semantic, 24
   semantic, 25
   signal, 27
reactive, 57
realism primitive,
references, 93
relating, 54
   levels, 61
relations, 1
relational abstracting, 59
relational language, 10
relativity, 13, 23, 59
   plus, 71
   principle of linguistic, 19
   theory, 19
reproductive system (See human)
reverse discrimination, 78
rigidification, 27
rigor, 56, 62
rigorous, 56
   analysis, 56
   language, 21
   logic,

meticulous, 57
meticulous analysis, 58, 62
qualitative, 48
qualitative analysis, 19, 60
qualitative meticulous, 41
qualitative meticulous analysis, 73
qualitative process,
root metaphor, 32, 73
   contextual, 23, 33
   mechanism, 27
   organicism, 24
Rosenberg, Duska, xi
Rousseau, 36
Russell, Bertrand, xxi, 37

science, 2, 3, 27, 50
   cybernetics, 26, 28
   natural, 27
   physics, 2
   social, 8, 26, 63
Science and Sanity, 20
scientific, 10, 60
   evidence, 52
   method, 63, 75
   process,
   research, 24
   theory, 8
secondary correspondence, 9
Secrets of the Universe, 21
segregation, 80
selection process, 76
self,
   actualizing, 79
   analysis, 28
   awareness, 29
   commentary, 84
   consciousness of, 27
   controlling, 31
   correcting, 27

Dr. William J. Williams

diagnosis, 79
examination, 29
expanding, 38
maintaining, 29
monitoring, 37, 39
moving, 29, 33
reflexive, 38
regulating, 34
self-correcting process, xviii
self-reflexive, xvii
  human, 39
  map, 47
semantics,
  blockage, 4
  primitive reaction, 29
  process, 8
  reaction, 25
  state, 65
  transactions, 79
sensing, 33
  stage, 33
  type, 59, 78
seventeenth century format, 27
seventeenth century machine model, 71
seventeenth century processes, 64
sexuality (See human sexuality)
signal reactions,
Simpson, Alan, 81
situation,
  law of, 79
  understanding, 26
  social, 23
    groups, 20
    science, 8
soft mathematics,
space/time, 10, 23, 25
Spinoza, 31
static, 29
  framework, 29

structure, 82
thinking, 11
world, 69
stereotype, 59
stimulus-response model, 26
structural, 3
  correspondence, 3
  gap, 10
  method, 76
  more, 25, 58
  process, 39
  similarity, 14, 47
  similarity correspondence, 10
  similarity external world, 2
  similarity world of events, 1
structure, 14
  clockwork, 28
  correspondence, 40
  dynamic, 24
  grammatical, 19
  internal thinking,
  language, 6, 9
  linear, 53
  mathematics, 12
  mechanical, 11
  natural, 3
  nervous, 2
  nervous system, 46
  semantic state, 3
  static, 26
  world, 8
styles, 83
  abstracting (See abstracting-styles)
subject, 53, 59
  linking-verb-adjective, 20
  linking-verb-noun, 20
  linking-verb-predicate-adjective, 21
  predicate, 54, 57

predicate language, 20
predicate-adjective, 21
verb-object,
submicroscopic, 13
  process, 13
  stirrings, 14
survivality, 13
syllogistic, 60
syllogistic reasoning, 31
symbiotic, 27
symbolic correspondence, 41
symbols, 45, 47
synthesis, 59
synthetic emergings, 9
synthetic theory, 26
systematization, 28, 32
systemization, 3, 71

tax policy, 7
map (See map-territory)
The Conceptual Revolutions,
theoretical-analytical, 10
theoretician, 27
theoria Greek, 24
theory,
  aggregates, 10
  analytical, 40
  construction,
  correspondence, 1
  electrical, 28
  evolution, 29
  fixed, 29
  function, 8, 11
  groups, 10
  local causes, 7
  mechanical matter,
  multiplier, 19
  Newtonian, 20
  nonidentity, 21
  nonlinear, 14

probability, 23
quantum, 24
relativity, 7
scientific, 7
synthetic, 24
types, 4
universal gravitation, 28
world, 31
thermodynamics, 32, 151
thermostat, 29
thinking, 29
  about thinking, 23, 40, 78
  analytical, 46
  Aristotelian, 70
  common sense, 16
  early Greek, 27
  fixed, 29
  formistic, 39
  fragmentary, 38
  how to think, 81
  levels, 60
  mechanical, 13, 18
  new, 10
  nonlogical, 11
  old, 23
  orders, 53
  organimistic,
  pre-Aristotelian, 27
  pre-rationality, 67
  primary, 56
  process, 28
  self-reflexive, 39
  static, 59
  vertical, 27
Thomas, Clarence, 31
time/space, 45
time-binding, 42
totality,
  illegitimate, 9
  legitimate, 9

transactions, 13
  notion of, 14, 15, 56
  process, 57
  semantics, 62
  vital, 57
transcursive,
transformation, 2, 10
translation, 39
treaties of government, 33
truth, 19, 23
Turner, Ted, 85
type,
  postulating (See postulating-type)
Types,
  abstracting (See abstracting-types)
  classifying (See classifying types)
  evaluating (See evaluating types)
  relating (See relating types)
  sensing (See sensing types)
  theory, 7

U.S. Constitution, 9, 23
undergirding, 10, 11
  epistemological, 19
  process, 9, 12
underpinnings,
  epistemological, 9, 69
unifying, 59
  abstracting, 59
  experience, 95
  levels, 59
unity,
  creative, 71
  character, 14, 43
  flux, 44
universal gravitation theory, 43

universality, 27
unspeakable level, 9

validity, 4
values, 48
  and weights, 48
variable, 16
  dependent (See dependent variable), 51
  independent (See independent variable), 49
  meanings, 50
verb-to-be, 20, 21
  fundamental focus, 19
vertical, 9
  focus, 7
  representation, 6
vicious circle, 4
vital transaction, 59

war, 77
water, 41
  drops of water analogy, 42
  fluoride, 43
weights, 3
  and values, 3
West (See East and West)
what,
  the what primary, 27
wheel,
  of fate, 23
  of fortune, 27, 28
wholeness, 24
Whorf, Benjamin Lee, 19
why, xxiii
  of abstracting, 11
  questions, 12
  use of,
WIGO, 45
Wittgenstein, Ludwig, 62
world,

a priori aspects, 10
common sense, 11
empirical, 3
external, 47
hypothesis, 38
nonlinear, 9
of degrees, 65
of Logical Positivism, 54
structural similarity, 10
structure, 2
theory, 33
understanding of, 8
view, 23, 36